SEVENTY-EIGHT
DEGREES OF
WISDOM

An in-depth analysis of the symbolism and psychological
resonances of the Tarot suit cards, including instructions
on how to give readings.

By the same author
SEVENTY-EIGHT DEGREES OF WISDOM
  PART 1: The Major Arcana
TAROT: THE OPEN LABYRINTH

SEVENTY-EIGHT DEGREES OF WISDOM

A BOOK OF TAROT

Part 2: The Minor Arcana and Readings

Rachel Pollack

THE AQUARIAN PRESS
Wellingborough, Northamptonshire

First published May 1983
Second Impression October 1983
Third Impression March 1984
Fourth Impression October 1984
Fifth Impression July 1985
Sixth Impression April 1986

British Library Cataloguing in Publication Data

Pollack, Rachel
    Seventy eight degrees of wisdom
    pt.2. Minor arcana and readings
    1. Tarot   2. Symbolism(Psychology)
    I. Title
    133.3′ 2424   BF 1879.T2
    ISBN 0-8530-339-7

*Cards from the Rider-Waite Tarot deck reproduced by permission
of the Hutchinson Publishing Group Limited*

The Aquarian Press is part of the Thorsons Publishing Group

Printed and bound in Great Britain

Contents

For Joan Goldstein, who knows that the best cards are the ones that tell the truth.

Introduction

THE RIDER PACK

In 1910 the Rider Company of London published a new Tarot deck, designed by the well-known occultist Arthur Edward Waite, and drawn by a lesser-known psychic artist named Pamela Colman Smith. Waite himself apparently did not expect a wide public for these new cards; like all his works, his book on the Tarot speaks primarily to people already involved in the occult tradition. And yet the Rider pack, as the deck came to be called, is now known all over the world – in its original version, in pirate editions, in thinly disguised 'new' Tarots, in several different sizes published by Rider alone, in illustrations for novels, books on psychology, comic books and television shows. The outstanding popularity of this particular esoteric Tarot over hundreds of other traditional and modern decks derives largely from one aspect of the cards that Waite himself seems hardly to have noticed – the drawings of Pamela Colman Smith which revolutionized the Minor Arcana.

In his apologia for his deck Waite took great pains to defend certain changes he made in the design and number of the cards in the Major Arcana. However, most newcomers to Tarot, comparing the Rider pack (centre, above) to say, the more traditional Marseilles deck (left, above) will have to look quite closely before they observe most of these changes. They will immediately see the difference in the Minor cards. In every deck designed before the Rider pack the 'pip' cards, numbers 1-10 of the four suits, bear geometric patterns containing the number of swords, or wands, or cups, or coins. In this they resemble their descendants, ordinary playing cards. In most decks these patterns are plain and repetitious. The elaborate Crowley deck (right, above) stands out as the exception. The Waite-Smith deck, however, has an illustration on every card.

Primarily concerned with the more esoteric Major cards, Waite apparently did not realize how this rich variety of scenes would captivate the average viewer seeking to experiment with Tarot. In a way, their very newness adds to their charm. Where the Major Arcana strikes us with the ancientness as well as the complexity of its symbolism, the Minor cards, having no pictorial tradition, appear to us as scenes taken directly from life, or in some cases, fantasy.

The fact that Smith drew these scenes in a pseudo-mediaeval style seems not to bother most people. They find the liveliness more important. Almost all the Major cards show a figure sitting or standing; only the Fool and the World move. In fact, they dance. But in the Minor cards, all the scenes show something *happening*, rather like a frame from a movie.

The contrast is no accident. The Major cards depict archetypal forces rather than real people. The Fool and the World Dancer move, because only they fully embody these principles. But the Minor cards show aspects of life as people actually live it. In these four suits, and more especially in the combinations they form when we lay them out in readings, we find a panorama of experience, constantly showing us new insights into the wonders of human nature and this magical world.

Precisely because it shows ordinary life rather than a formal system the Rider pack does not appeal to many occultists. While a great many subsequent decks have copied, with small or large variations, the Rider pack, other decks, including ones we might characterize as 'most serious', such as the Crowley or the Builders of the Adytum deck, have returned to the use of patterns for the pip cards. They do so because their creators concerned themselves with the Tarot as a system of organizing and structuring esoteric practices, both as a tool and as a living force. The Tarot, for them, forms a vital link to mystical systems.

The most important of these links is that connecting the four suits to the four worlds described in the Qabalah. Qabalists view the universe as existing in four stages, the closest to us (and the furthest from direct union with God) being the ordinary material world, called Assiyah, the 'World of Action'. For greater understanding the mediaeval theosophists described each world as embodied in a Tree of Life, a diagram of cosmic law. Now, the structure of the Tree does not change in the different worlds. Each tree contains ten Sephiroth, or archetypes of emanation. (For the Tree's most common pattern, see the Ten of Pentacles.) And here, of course, the Tarot comes in. Because the four suits each contain ten pip cards, we can place the cards on the Sephiroth to give us a concrete aid in meditation. And because the Sephiroth represent archetypal forces, most occultists prefer abstract designs to emblemize them. For them, a scene of people doing something, such as three women dancing, or a group of boys fighting, only distracts from the eternal symbolism.

Some occultists go further, believing that the geometric patterns on the cards carry a psychic power all their own, and that by looking deeply at these patterns in their special colours, we can produce certain distinct effects within the brain.

Many people who are not especially esotericists will still prefer the older decks to any of the modern interpretations, including the geometric ones. For them, the sense of a tradition, of meanings developed over centuries, carries a power no revised edition can equal. In readings they look to the ancient formulas and find the Rider pack's detailed scenes a distraction. Often the more psychic readers will use the older cards, finding that the very abstractness of the pip cards helps trigger clairvoyant awareness.

For most of us, however, the repetitious patterns sharply limit the insights available from either studying the cards alone or using them in readings. Once we have memorized the formulas attached to each card we find it difficult to go further. In this book I have attempted to create what I call a 'humanistic' Tarot, derived not just from esoteric truths, but also from the insights of modern post-Jungian psychology to give a rounded picture of who we are, how we act, and what forces shape and direct us. In such a Tarot the goal is not fixed meanings, but rather a *method* by which each person can gain a greater insight into life. While the analysis of each card will come partly from its use in readings, with right side up and reversed meanings, the analysis will show primarily how that card adds to our knowledge of human experience.

Because the Rider pack shows such vivid scenes the formulas or commentaries belonging to each card serve only as starting points. We can ponder the pictures themselves, and how they combine with the pictures around them. In a way the pictures and each person's imagination (and experience) act as a partnership. In every reading, or in each meditation or reflection, we can look at each card as a fresh experience. Just as the more esoteric decks work best for occult discipline, and the older decks for fortune-telling, so the Rider serves those of us who use the cards primarily for awareness of self and of the world around us.

The Smith pictures attract people through their cartooon-like action. They hold us over years because of the very real meanings contained in their pictures. How did Pamela Smith do it? As far as we know, she created her pictures with no tradition to assist her. In Part One of this book I stated my opinion that Waite probably did not dictate the designs as he clearly did with the Major cards. His own book gives no account of their origins; nor does he defend the radical change, as he does his changes in the Major cards. His interpretations, moreover, do not utilize the new pictures to any great extent. Though he briefly describes each picture his explanations are usually formulas and catch phrases ('desire, will, determination, project'), no different in substance from those meanings attached to earlier decks.

Some writers have claimed (though I have not found any evidence for this in Waite's own writings) that Smith drew the pictures as four comic book-like stories, one for each suit. The quality of the suit determined the character of the story, in which the court cards formed a family and the pips events happening to them. The so-called Moroccan Tarot, based very closely on the Rider pack, follows this system. This story explanation for the pictures begs the question. The important question remains the relation of the picture to the meaning.

I suspect Waite gave Smith the formulas he wished illustrated, perhaps consulted with her on the picture, and then Smith's artistic instincts took over, at times working with the surface symbolism and at times operating beyond the level of conscious choice. Waite's formulas derive from various sources. Waite himself speaks at times of contradictory meanings, as if he had consulted different fortune-tellers. His arrangement of the court cards also shows the influence of the Order of the Golden Dawn, a secret society of mystic magicians, to which Waite and Smith (like Crowley and Paul Foster Case, designer of the BOTA deck) at one time belonged.

In many cases, of course, the pictures are very simple and directly related to the meanings they were meant to illustrate. The Four of Pentacles, for example, shows the image of a miser, someone 'cleaving' to the 'surety of possessions'. But is it coincidence or plan that these four pentacles cover the crown of the head, the heart and throat, and the soles of the feet, thereby leading to deeper interpretations than simple greed? And in many cases, the picture touches something in us beyond the meaning officially connected to it. Look at the Six of Swords, supposedly a 'journey by water'. The dream-like silence, the sadness implicit in the picture suggest the mythical journey of dead souls across the River Styx.

I do not mean to describe Waite as bland, or insensitive to the pictures in his own deck. Sometimes his comments, especially on the pictures, increase our understanding beyond the simple list of meanings. In that Six of Swords he observes that 'the freight is light', and this, along with Eden Gray's comment, 'The swords do not weigh down the boat', leads us to contemplate the image of a spiritual or emotional journey in which we carry our memories and sorrows with us. In the Two of Wands Waite gives two opposed meanings and then says that the picture 'gives a clue' to their resolution. At other times, however, the meaning given contradicts the picture, as in the Two of Swords, where a powerful image of isolation and defence supposedly illustrates 'friendship'.

Since the Rider pack quite a few Tarot designers have attempted to include a scene on every card. Just about all have paid tribute to Pamela Smith's images, some extremely closely, while others have imaginatively transformed the Rider pictures. Nothing compels them to use these images; they carry no authority of ancient tradition, as do the Major cards. Their authority derives from creative achievement. These crudely drawn pictures, awkward, often out of all proportion or perspective, based on sentimental ideas of the Middle Ages, somehow have led thousands of people into an understanding not just of the cards but of themselves. In one stroke Pamela Smith created a new tradition.

THE FOUR SUITS

However much the depiction of the individual cards broke with previous practice, Waite stayed close to earlier decks in his arrangement of the suits and their emblems – with one exception. Where older decks, going all the way back to the fifteenth-century Visconti-Sforza deck, used Wands (or Staves), Cups, Swords, and Coins (or discs), the Rider pack substituted Pentacles – five pointed stars enclosed in gold discs – for the final suit. Waite made this change for two reasons. First, he wanted his fourth suit to represent the full range of the physical world, not simply the narrow materialism of money and business. Second, he wanted the four suits to carry the four basic tools of ritual magic. In reality the two reasons are one. Waite knew that magicians used these objects partly because they symbolized in concrete form the various aspects of the physical/spiritual universe.

The association of these four emblems with both magical practice and the spiritual truth underlying life goes back at least as far the the Middle Ages, where we find their equivalents in the symbolic objects carried by the Grail maidens. Waite himself knew these objects from his experience in magical Orders. The Rider pack also depicts them as lying on the table before the Magician in the Major Arcana.

In the Tarot, as in magic, the four emblems stand for the world itself and for human nature, as well as the act of creation (both the creation of specific *things,* and the continuous creation of evolution). Their place on the Magician's table signifies that he or she has become a master of the physical world. In one sense mastery means the real powers over nature that many people seek in magic. Those who use the Tarot as an esoteric discipline sometimes maintain that meditation and ritual with the Minor Arcana will give the adept control over the forces of nature. In Charles William's Tarot novel, *The Greater Trumps,* he carries this idea to dramatic extremes when the hero raises a hurricane by flapping together the cards associated with wind. In psychological terms 'mastery' of the Minor Arcana means understanding, in ourselves and in the world around us, all those experiences and forces depicted in the cards. A 'master' means a person who has control over his or her life – who is master over him or herself.

Such a goal is a great deal harder to achieve than many people might think. It means really knowing who we are, on unconscious levels as well as conscious. It means knowing why we act the way we do, knowing our true desires instead of the muddled ideas most people have of their goals in life. It means knowing the connections between seemingly random experiences. The Tarot can at least help us increase our understanding in all these things. How far each person goes depends on, among other things, that person's relationship to the cards.

The number four has figured very strongly in human attempts to understand existence. Because our bodies suggest this number (front and back, right and left sides) we tend to organize our perceptions of the ever shifting world by breaking things down into fours. The view of the year as four seasons comes also from the two solstices and the two equinoxes. (Cultures without astronomical awareness will often divide the year into the two basic seasons of summer and winter, or sometimes into three seasons.)

The zodiac contains twelve constellations, three times four. Therefore we find the signs of astrology divided into four groups of three. One 'fixed' sign in each group gives us the four 'strong points' of heaven. We see these four represented in the Major Arcana on the cards of the World and the Wheel of

Fortune as the four beasts shown in the cards' four corners. (The very shape of cards, and for that matter most Western houses, demonstrates our four-sided bias. The ancient Chinese used circular playing cards.) The four creatures symbolize the zodiac, but they derive most directly from Ezekiel's vision in the Old Testament, later repeated in Revelation.

Of all the four symbolisms the two that pertain most directly to the Minor Arcana are the four elements of mediaeval alchemy and the four letters of God's name in Hebrew, the tetragrammaton. Our modern concept of the atomic elements derives from an earlier idea (originating in ancient Greece) that all things in nature are formed out of four basic constituents: fire, water, air, and earth. We find this idea not just in Europe but also in cultures as diverse as China and North America. The elements sometimes change; sometimes the numbers change also, from four to five, adding 'ether' or Spirit to the four elements of nature (just as many cultures add the 'centre' as a fifth direction). The basic concept, however, remains the same – that everything can be reduced to its basic parts, that the world combines these basic qualities in an infinity of ways.

Today, we carry this idea much further, reducing all matter to sub-atomic particles (throwing out the idea of Spirit altogether, except in certain rarefied theories of contemporary physics) and looking upon the mediaeval 'elements' as very elaborate chemical combinations. However, we are mistaken if we think that the old system can no longer teach us anything. For one thing that characterizes the old view – and indeed the views of virtually all cultures before the modern West – is the non-separation of physical, spiritual, moral, and psychological theories and values. For us the element of, say, helium, carries very little if any spiritual meaning. For the mediaeval thinkers the element Fire suggested a whole range of associations. Obviously we would be wrong to reject the great achievements of knowledge we call modern science. But neither should we reject the insights from earlier times.

In the Tarot we see the four elements as Fire-Wands (Staves), Water-Cups, Air-Swords, Earth-Pentacles (Coins). Different writers sometimes give variations on this listing, most often switching Wands and Pentacles, on the grounds that sticks grow out of the earth, and coins are forged in a fire. I have chosen to stay with the more common listing because of the wider associations of fire and earth. Fire is not simply a human tool, but a great force in nature, seen most powerfully in the sun which brings the staves out of the ground. Earth stands not only for the soil, but traditionally for the entire material universe of which Coins represent a small part and Pentacles a much wider part.

If we wish to see the world in terms of five rather than four, including Spirit centre, then the Major Arcana stands for Ether, the fifth element. The fact that we set it apart from the four Minor elements symbolizes the intuition that Spirit somehow exists on a different level from the ordinary world. At the same time the fact that we mix all five together for readings helps us see that in reality Spirit and all the elements of matter constantly work together. Working with the Tarot helps us understand the dynamic ways in which Spirit gives meaning and unity to the material world. A true understanding of this relationship, in practice as well as theory, forms a great step towards that 'mastery' described earlier.

Many people will know the imagery of the four elements from astrology, with its four 'triplicities': Fire – Aries, Leo, Sagittarius; Water – Cancer, Scorpio, Pisces; Air – Gemini, Libra, Aquarius; Earth – Taurus, Virgo, Capricorn. Jungian psychology also utilizes the four elements, linking them to basic ways of experiencing the world. Fire stands for Intuition, Water for Feeling, Air for Thinking, and Earth for Sensation.

In astrology and Jungian thought the elements stand for types and characteristics. In the Tarot we see these types reflected in the court cards. The suits as a whole show activities and qualities of life rather than individual psychology. In other words, if Wands dominate in a reading we do not say that the person is a 'fiery' character, but rather that she or he is currently going through many Fire experiences. We study the four suits separately to learn just what we mean by Fire or Water or Air or Earth experience. We study them together in readings to learn how life in reality embraces and combines all the elements together.

As a brief summary, Wands/Fire stand for action, movement, optimism, adventure, struggle, business in the sense of the activity of commerce rather than the things sold, beginnings. Cups/Water stand for reflection, quiet experiences, love, friendship, joy, fantasy, passivity. Swords/Air stand for conflict, angry or disturbed emotions, sadness, but

also for mental activity, wisdom, the use of intellect to under-stand the truth. Pentacles/Earth stand for nature, money, work, routine activities, stable relationships, business in the sense of things made and sold. Also, because Pentacles are magic signs, they stand for the magic of nature and the wonder of ordinary life, not always perceived, but often hidden under the surface.

Drawing on another well-known symbolic system Wands and Swords represent 'yang' or 'active' situations, while Cups and Pentacles stand for 'yin' or 'passive' ones. We can also substitute, with reference to the Major Arcana, Magician for yang and High Priestess for yin. Whatever the terminology, these distinctions become clearer in the imagery. Both wands and swords are used for striking; cups, on the other hand, fulfil their function by receiving and holding water; while pentacles, as either magic signs or money, can influence the world without physically moving. Similarly, fire and air are constantly shifting, while water and earth tend more to inertia.

A little reflection, as well as a look at the pictures, will show how these separate categories actually blend together in reality. Both Wands and Pentacles deal with business, both Wands and Swords indicate conflict. Cups and Wands tend towards happy, positive experiences, while Pentacles and Swords often represent the more difficult sides of life. At the same time, Cups and Swords cover the general range of emotions, while Pentacles and Wands depict the more physical activities. Rather than showing rigid separations the cards tend toward combinations and the blurring of all distinctions.

In Part One I wrote that the study of Tarot readings teaches us above all that no quality is good or bad except within the context of an actual situation. We learn also from readings that no situation, quality, or personal characteristic exists in isolation, but only in combination with others. In a reading we look first at the individual cards in their individual positions, but we understand what the reading tells us when we see how the cards blend together into a whole pattern. Similarly, we study the cards individually but we understand them fully only when we see them working.

The different elements represent not only different experiences but also different approaches to life. One reason to study the suits as a whole is to see the advantages and problems of each approach. For each suit we will look at a 'problem' and a 'Way to Spirit'. As an example, the problem for Cups is passivity, the Way to Spirit is love. Through the different images we see how the Cups experiences bring out these qualities.

In arranging the cards I have followed Waite's example in moving from the King down to the Ace, rather than the other way round. Because kings (as traditional symbols rather than political reality) bear a responsibility for maintaining society, and because the king gives an image of maturity, the four Kings all symbolize the most socially-minded stable version of the suit. The Aces, on the other hand, signify unity and perfection. Therefore, the Aces stand for the elements in their purest form. The Ace of Wands stands for Fire itself and all that it means, while the other thirteen Wands cards depict some specific example of Fire, either in a situation (cards 2 - 10) or as a personality type (the court cards).

In the Rider pack we see each Ace held in a hand coming out of a cloud. This symbol, seen also in other decks, teaches us that each element can lead us to spiritual mystery. It also teaches us that all experience is a gift, from a source we cannot consciously know, unless we follow the deep spiritual journey shown in the Major Arcana. For this reason I have ended each suit with the Ace.

THE TETRAGRAMMATON

Besides the four elements we should look at the other symbol implied by the four suits, that of God's name. We find these four letters, Yod-Heh-Vav-Heh, arranged in the Wheel of Fortune, the tenth card of the Major Arcana. In European letters we write them as YHVH, or sometimes IHVH. Because the Bible gives no vowels for the name we cannot actually pronounce it; it therefore symbolizes God's unknowable nature, the essential separation between God and man that characterizes Western religion. Writers have assigned the names Jehovah or Jah or Yahweh to those letters, but this leads to confusion. When we consult the writings of the Qabalists we discover that the letters do not form a 'name' in the human sense of a label that stands for a person, but rather they depict a formula. And that formula describes the process of creation.

The tetragrammaton and the four elements do not really form two separate systems, but in fact one unified symbol. Each of the elements belongs to a letter, Yod-Fire, Heh-Water, Vav-Air, Heh-Earth,* and when we apply God's name to the elements we complete the meaning of their symbolic differences.

The process goes as follows: Yod, or Fire, symbolizes the start of any enterprise, the first creative spark, the energy needed to begin. In mythic terms the Yod indicates the divine spark emerging from the unknowable God. In psychological terms it stands for the impulse to begin some specific project, or new way of life. The first Heh, Water, symbolizes the actual beginning as the spark is 'received' into a pattern. Mythically, this refers to God's Fire touching the 'Waters of the deep', that is, the chaos before God began to order the universe. Psychologically we understand that our plans and hopes remain formless, vague, until the Fire energy enters into them and starts us actually doing something. At the same time, restless Wands energy cannot benefit us unless we give it a definite purpose.

The third letter, Vav, connected to Air, symbolizes the development of the plan, the directed purposeful movement that makes everything take shape. In its holy sense, it means the stage of creation in which God gave the world its underlying form. Air stands for intellect, and psychologically Vav indicates the mental process of going from a goal to an actual plan which will bring the project into reality.

Finally, the second Heh, Earth, stands for the finished creation, the thing itself. In religious terms it means matter, the physical universe, that which God created through the process of the other letters. In human terms it means the completion of the goal.

Let us take the example of a poem. It cannot begin without an impulse towards poetry and a desire to express something. At the same time this desire goes nowhere unless we can choose a particular subject. In a sense the subject 'receives' the impulse to write. Still, the poem will never emerge until we work on it, using intellect and the writing of several drafts to solve the problems of imagery, rhythm, and so on. Finally, the

*These links come from Tarot tradition. Some Qabalists use a slightly different order.

process ends when we can hold the actual poem in our hands and pass it on to others. A little thought will show that the same development holds true for any action, from building a house to brewing beer to making love.

Clearly the last element, Earth, stands somewhat apart from the others. The mathematician and occultist, P. D. Ouspensky, has drawn this relationship in the following diagram:

A look at the Hebrew letters will also help us understand the symbolism. Reading right to left they are:

Notice how the Yod, the Fire letter, hardly has any shape at all, but resembles rather a point, the flash of a first impulse. Observe too that the two Hehs vaguely resemble upside down cups, or beakers. The first one 'receives' the impulse, the second 'receives' the entire process and gives it a physical form. Finally, observe how the third letter, Vav, extends the first letter, Yod. The intellect, Air, takes the Fire energy and gives it a definite direction.

It may seem at first that the fourth element, Earth, can exist by itself. However, in order for us to find any meaning in our possessions we must understand the creative processes that brought them into being. When we look at the 'problems' relating to each suit, we see that each arises only when we remove the suit from its relationship to the others. Or, in other words, when we lean too much in one direction in life. Earth's problem of materialism, is counteracted through adding Cups, for emotional appreciation. The way in which one suit is 'added' to another will be discussed in the section on Readings.

THE GATE CARDS

If the Rider Minor cards serve us primarily as a commentary on ordinary life, they do not ignore or cut us off from deeper perceptions. On the contrary, the philosophical bias of the cards leads us always in the direction of 'hidden forces' giving shape and meaning to ordinary experience. A truly realistic view of the world (as opposed to the narrow materialist ideology commonly thought of as 'realism') will recognize the spiritual energy always present within the constantly shifting patterns of the world. Much of mainstream science is currently moving away from the notion that such forces as electro-magnetism are static and mechanical, and towards the image of them as dynamic and constantly creative.

The Rider pack greatly encourages such awareness. We see it celebrated in the Ten of Cups; we see it most directly in the Aces, where each element is shown as a gift.

But the Rider pack does more than *teach* us this awareness. Certain cards, taken in the right way, can help produce it. Earlier, we considered the occult view that looking at geometric patterns will create effects in the brain. In a similar way joining ourselves meditatively to particular cards in the four suits will bring experiences reaching beyond the cards' specific meanings.

I call these cards Gates, because of the way in which they open a path from the ordinary world to the inner level of archetypal experiences. Each suit contains at least one of these cards, the Pentacles containing the most. They all share certain characteristics: complex, often contradictory, meanings, and a mythlike Strangeness which no allegorical interpretation can completely penetrate. By choosing certain cards to fulfil this function I do not mean to imply that no others will do so, but only that in my experience these cards in particular do act in this way.

Sometimes the Strangeness of a Gate will lie on the surface, but in other cards it only becomes apparent after we have analysed the card intellectually. The latter cases demonstrate a very important point – that outer and inner perceptions do not oppose each other, but rather bring each other out. The best approach to a Gate card begins with a knowledge of the card's literal and symbolic meanings. When we have taken those as far as they will go we will arrive at the path of

Strangeness that lies beyond them.

The Tarot demonstrates many things, some very unexpect-ed. These things emerge through interpretation of the Tarot's images, through joining ourselves to those images in medita-tion, and through seeing the combinations formed in readings. Taken separately, the cards of the Minor Arcana present us with a grand panorama of human experiences. Together, and in union with the archetypal Major cards, they draw us into ever wider knowledge of the changing wonder of life.

THE MINOR ARCANA

Chapter I.

Wands

In one way or another, human beings have taken virtually all of nature as symbols for the spiritual essence of life. Of all these symbols fire stands out as the most powerful. We speak of the 'divine spark' in the soul, of someone being 'on fire with an idea', and when someone has become bitter or disillusioned we say, 'the fire has gone out of him'. When God banished Adam and Eve from the Garden of Eden and its Tree of Life He set a cherub with a flaming sword to guard the entrance. By their Fall the first humans had alienated themselves from the heavenly fire. When yogis, through meditation and exercise, cause the kundalini, or spiritual force, to rise, they experience this rising as a great heat moving up the spine. And shamans the world over demonstrate their spiritual power by becoming masters of fire, dancing in flames or holding hot coals in their mouths.

Fire stands for the vital life essence that animates our bodies. Without it we become corpses. Michelangelo's famous painting of creation shows a spark leaping from God's finger to Adam's. We describe the chemical changes of food in our stomachs as the body 'burning fuel'. Fire symbolizes the very energy of existence. Because it rises, constantly leaping upwards, fire stands for optimism, confidence, hope. To give human beings a touch of immortality and make them immune to Zeus's threats of annihilation, Prometheus gave them fire.

Because the Minor Arcana deals primarily with the outer range of experience Wands tend to show the way the inner fire shows itself in ordinary life. Besides the specific knowledge gained, a study of the Minor Arcana shows how mundane experience derives from a spiritual base.

Wands, then, stand first of all for movement. Whether they win or lose Wands constantly struggle, not so much because of the actual problems or goals, but just for the love of conflict, of the chance to use all that energy. In business Wands stand for commerce and competition; in love they symbolize romance, proposals, the act of winning a lover rather than the emotion of love itself. Wands lead us to approach life with action and eagerness.

When Wands succeed too greatly, as with the King, or the figure in Two, then a melancholy can grip them, for the rewards of success can tie them down. At other times, as in the Nine or Ten, they allow the habit of fighting or of taking on all problems, to blind them to more peaceful alternatives.

Mostly, however, the Wands' influence shows us people winning their battles. Through Wands we find the Way to Spirit in movement, action, living for the joy of living. They find their most powerful expression in the Four, dancing out of the walled city to celebrate the lifegiving power of the Sun.

And yet, for all that vitalizing energy expressed in the Sun's power to literally bring life out of the ground, fire also destroys. If not controlled and directed, that energy burns up the world. Therefore we see all the Wands court cards standing or sitting in a desert. Despite their optimism and eagerness Wands need the softening influence of Cups, for without water the summer sun brings only a drought. From Cups, then, comes a sense of depth and the ability to feel as well as act. From Swords we get a sense of planning and direction for all the energy. From Swords also comes an awareness of sorrow and pain to balance the Wands' optimism and conquering spirit. And from Pentacles comes a sense of being rooted in the real world, an ability to enjoy life as well as to overcome it.

Figure 1

KING

In readings, the court cards of each suit traditionally represent people who will influence the subject's life. While this is often the case, they can also symbolize the subject him or herself. Taken by themselves, that is, outside the context of specific readings, the sixteen court cards provide a greater range of human character. Either in a reading or by itself as an object of study any specific court card indicates a person having or expressing those qualities signified by that card.

A King (or a Knight or a Page) does not necessarily mean a man, nor a Queen a woman. Rather, they show qualities and attitudes traditionally symbolized by those figures. The particular social functions of a king, or a queen, or a knight, suggest certain experiences and responsibilities. The cards symbolize these as often as they stand for age or sex.

We should also avoid the idea that a card might symbolize an individual person throughout life, in the sense of saying about someone, 'She's the Queen of Wands', and thinking that sums up her life. A person might go through a Queen of Swords phase one month, and move to a Knight of Cups the next. Or experience both at once, in different aspects of her life at that time.

A king is a ruler, responsible for the welfare of society. In the Rider pack all four Kings wear what Waite calls 'a cap of maintenance' underneath their crowns. Traditionally the king bears responsibility for maintaining his people. Therefore, all the Kings represent both success (for the king, after all, is supreme) and social responsibility.

The King of Wands translates these qualities into Wands terms. He indicates a strong-minded person, able to dominate others by strength of will. His power derives from a firm belief in his own rightness. He *knows* the truth; he *knows* his method is best. He considers it only natural for others to follow him.

At the same time he shows the Wands energy controlled and turned into useful projects, or long-term careers. The adventurous Wands nature can make such a person uncomfortable in this role. He leans forward on his throne, as if he would like to leap up and go to seek new experience.

He is naturally honest, seeing no reason or value in lies. He is positive and optimistic for much the same reason; the Wands energy burns so strongly in him he does not understand why anyone would express negative attitudes.

Such a strong personality can tend towards intolerance, unable to understand weakness or despair because he has not experienced these things himself. This impatient side of the King might bear the motto, 'If I can do it you can'. Once, in a reading, I saw a very nice expression of what people used to call 'the generation gap': the King of Wands and the Fool, both of them energetic, yet one the essence of responsibility, the other the pure image of instinct and freedom.

Two symbols dominate the card: the lion, emblem of Leo, and the salamander, a legendary lizard believed to inhabit fire. They represent the mundane and the spiritual, for while Leo indicates the personality traits belonging to Fire, the salamander was a favourite symbol of the alchemists. At his best the King is master of the creative Fire. His sense of social commitment has tamed it and put it to use. Notice that the salamanders on his robe are shown with their tails in their mouths. The closed circle means maturity and completion.

Compare this image with the Knight's shirt, where the tails and mouths do not meet.

REVERSED

When we reverse a card we alter in some way its prime meaning, as if the original impact had become blocked or rechannelled, or, in some cases, liberated. Some Tarot commentators prefer to discount reversed meanings, and it is true that in meditation or creativity we usually consider all cards as right side up. But in readings or study reversed meanings do more than double the possible meanings in the deck. By showing us the card from a different angle they give us a wider understanding of what the card really means.

In a reading, if a court card refers to a specific person (by physical type, say, rather than the card's qualities), then reversed indicates that person disturbed or blocked, or maybe having a bad influence on the subject. If, on the other hand, we look at the qualities in the card then reversed shows those qualities altered.

Right side up the King shows us someone powerful and commanding, yet often intolerant of other people's weaknesses. Reversed we see that natural fire after it has encountered obstacles and defeats that might make a less forceful person cynical or frightened. Because he is the King of Wands he does not lose his force but becomes instead tempered, more understanding of others and at the same time harsher in his attitude to life, which no longer appears such an easy contest. Waite's formula here is very apt: 'Good but severe, austere yet tolerant'.

Figure 2

QUEEN

The Queen represents the yin, or receptive qualities of each element. She shows an appreciation of that element rather than the King's social use of it. This does not mean that the Queens indicate weakness, or even inaction, but rather the element translated into feeling and understanding.

Once again, we need not apply these qualities only to women. If, in a reading, we see the Queen as identifying a person by physical type alone, then the Queen naturally means a woman. But if we wish to apply the symbolic qualities to someone, then any court card can signify a woman or a man. And apart from readings the Queen of Wands stands for a particular appreciation of life.

In contrast with the King's eagerness and impatience, the Queen sits on her throne as if planted there. Her crown is flowering, her dress is sunshine. Alone of all the Queens she sits with her legs apart, signifying sexual energy. She shows a Fire appreciation of life, warm, passionate, very solidly in the world. Like the King, she is honest and sincere, seeing no purpose in deceit or nastiness. More sensitive than the King she allows herself to love both life and other people, seeing control or dominance as of no more value than cynicism.

A black cat guards her throne. In Christian folklore the Devil gave a black cat to a witch to guard her from attack. The meaning here is less melodramatic. Sometimes if a person loves life, the world appears to respond by protecting that person from harm and sending her or him joyous experiences. We cannot understand the way in which this happens without reaching the complex and inner knowledge of the universe symbolized by the last cards of the Major Arcana. Nevertheless it can happen, and the black cat shows this response by nature to someone who approaches it with fiery joy.

REVERSED

As with the King the upside down Queen shows the reaction of such a person to opposition and sorrow. The basic good nature and positive attitudes of the Queen, as well as her energy, make her invaluable in a crisis or disaster. We can see her as the kind of person who will take over the running of someone's house when they have had a crisis and at the same time offer advice, consultation, emotional support, all these things coming from a natural impulse rather than any sense of duty.

At the same time this good nature demands that life respond in a positive way. Too much disaster or too much opposition from life (and the weakness of such a person can be a tendency to think of life as 'unfair'), and a nasty streak can emerge. She can become deceitful, jealous, unfaithful, or somewhat bitter.

Figure 3

KNIGHT

The Knights translate the quality of each suit into movement. The energy we saw as accomplishment in the King, and awareness in the Queen, here bursts forth at an earlier stage. In the Knights we see the ways in which each element is put to use. At the same time, the Knights lack the sureness and stability of the Kings and Queens.

Because Fire itself symbolizes movement, the Knight of Wands shows this quality in the extreme. In the words of some commentators he is 'Fire of Fire' or 'Fire exalted'. He represents eagerness, action, movement for its own sake, adventure and travel. Without some grounding influence all this excitement can dissipate itself as he tries to fly in every direction at once. Allied to a sense of purpose and aided by some Air-like influence of planning, the Knight of Wands can provide the energy and self-confidence for great achievement.

Notice that on his shirt the salamanders' tails do not touch their mouths, symbolizing incomplete action, unformed plans. In contrast to the King, the Knight has only begun his adventures.

REVERSED

Picture the young Knight. Unlike the experienced warrior he seeks battle at every opportunity, needing to prove his courage and strength, to himself and to others. And yet he is easily thrown from his horse. Untried, all that Wands and Knight eagerness carries a certain fragile quality. Opposition confuses him, even brings his great projects crashing down around him. Expecting everything to fall before him, he may find himself in basic disharmony with people or situations around him. His actions are interrupted as he finds his basic good nature at odds with people and situations. In a reading, therefore, the reversed Knight symbolizes confusion, disrupted projects, breakdown, and disharmony.

Figure 4

PAGE

The Pages represent the quality of each suit in its simplest state, enjoying itself for itself in a lighter, more youthful, way than the mature Queen. Physically, Pages refer to children. In relation to adults they indicate a moment when a person experiences some aspect of life just for itself, free of external pressures. As children, the Pages very often symbolize beginnings, study, reflection, the qualities of the young student.

Because Wands symbolize beginning, the Page of Wands especially indicates the start of projects, and in particular an announcement to the world, and to ourselves, that we are ready to begin either a 'project' (this can refer to a relationship as well as practical plans) or a new phase of life. On a simpler level the Page can represent a messenger, message or information. In emotional situations the Page's simple eagerness implies a faithful friend or lover.

REVERSED

Quieter than the Knight, the Page is not thrown so wildly by problems but instead becomes confused and indecisive. His eagerness to start is disrupted by complexities and outright opposition, leaving him afraid or unable to declare himself. Because his basic qualities are simplicity and faithfulness (notice that many of the salamanders on his suit are complete, signifying not finished projects as with the King, but rather a simple wholeness in the self), when indecisive he can become unstable and weak. A person indicated by this card needs either to get away from complexity or to develop the maturity to deal with it. Continued indecision can only lead to the resolve and self-confidence degenerating further.

Figure 5

TEN

Because they are so involved in movement and action the Wands invite problems. Constantly in conflict they almost attract enemies and difficulty. This comes partly from the lack of purpose and plan, but also from Wands' secret enjoyment of any contest.

The Ten shows us, on the surface, an image of a person burdened and oppressed by life, and especially by responsibility. His Wands eagerness has involved him in so many situations that now, paradoxically, that very energy is weighed down with commitments and problems. He wants to be free to travel, to seek adventure and new involvements; but instead he finds himself, like the suburban career man, caught in a net of endless responsibilities – financial, family, work – that he himself has created. He did not plan this; it has grown up around him.

We see here the great Wands problem. The Fire energy acts without thinking, takes on new problems simply for the challenge. But these situations and responsibilities do not go away when the person becomes bored and wants to go on to something new. They remain and can swamp the fire that seemed to conquer them.

In emotional situations the card shows us the person who takes on himself or herself all the weight of a relationship. Whatever problems arise, conflicts and dissatisfaction, he or she tries to smooth them over. With bent back she or he struggles to keep the relationship going, while the other person(s) may not even recognize what is happening.

In both the practical and the emotional situation the person has taken the burdens on her or himself. He or she has made the situation and needs to realize that other approaches are still possible. In such situations the burdens may not be wholly real, or at least may be avoided; they may in fact serve as an excuse to avoid doing anything really constructive such as breaking away from a bad situation.

REVERSED
Like many cards, especially when reversed, more than one meaning is possible. In a reading we can determine the best meaning (though sometimes more than one meaning will apply, as with a choice) partly through the other cards, and partly through an intuition that can only develop with practice. In study this variety of meanings demonstrates the fact that a situation can change in many ways.

Most simply the Ten of Wands reversed indicates that the burdens have increased in weight and number to the point where the person may collapse from them, physically or emotionally. At the same time it can mean that the person has thrown off the burdens (perhaps because they have become too much to bear). From here the situation branches again. Does he or she throw down the sticks because of a realization that he or she can use the energy to better purpose? Or does the person only rebel against the responsibilities without really doing anything constructive? A woman I once read for described it as a question of throwing the sticks behind or before us. If behind, we attempt a new direction. If before, it means we will pick them up again and continue trudging on the same road.

Figure 6

NINE

The Nines show how the suits deal with problems and the compromises they demand. Fire implies great strength, physical power, mental alertness. Emotionally, however, this predilection to fighting can trap Wands in patterns of conflicts. In the Nine we see again the image of someone who has faced a lot of opposition, from others and from life; rather than take it on himself, however, he has fought back. The act of fighting has developed his strength so that the picture shows someone muscular and keen-eyed. The Wands behind him can represent his resources in life, or else his problems looming up behind him. Either way, he is ready for the next fight.

Notice, however, his rigid posture, the stiffness and the raised shoulder. Notice also the bandage around his head, indicating a psychic wound. The battler is not a whole person. Whether by necessity or habit he has closed off awareness of life beyond conflict, and now looks only for the next fight, while his eyes see only the enemy, sometimes even after the enemy has surrendered.

REVERSED
Again, alternatives. First, the defence fails. The obstacles and problems grow too great for his strength to hold them back.

The other meaning, however, is that of looking for some different approach.

We should not assume the card always advises us to give up fighting. To abandon defensiveness means taking a great risk, for what happens if the problems we have kept at bay for so long rush up at us? Context is everything and sometimes the context demands those powerful shoulders and sharp eyes. And yet, observe how much energy the person uses up simply keeping himself tense and ready for battle. In specific readings the true implications of this card can only become clear through seeing it combine with other cards.

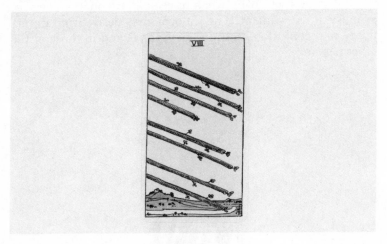

Figure 7

EIGHT

Fire implies swiftness and movement. Though this movement sometimes lacks direction we see here the image of a journey reaching an end, or things completed. When the Fire finds its goal, the projects and situations come to a satisfactory end. The Wands have come to earth. Therefore, the image on this card implies the addition of Pentacles grounding to Wands energy.

Romantically Waite calls them the 'arrows of love'. We can see this especially as meaning action taken in a love affair, seduction, or proposals made and accepted.

REVERSED

Turned around the image becomes one of continuance, of nothing coming to an end, especially when an end is desired. A situation or attitude simply goes on and on, with no conclusion in sight. If such a situation cannot be avoided, then it is good to recognize it and accept it, rather than let it bring frustration or disappointment. On the other hand, sometimes we ourselves can bring about this up-in-the-air quality by expecting a situation to remain unresolved. One of the most important positions in a reading is that called 'hopes and fears'; very often it turns out to be a self-fulfilling prophecy.

The arrows of love, when reversed, become arrows of jealousy and argument. The jealousy may derive from uncertainty and confusion, both in our feelings and in those of the other person.

Figure 8

SEVEN

Like the Nine, this is a card of conflict, but here we see the battle itself, and the effect is exhilarating. With their natural strength and positiveness Wands expect to win and usually do. Through active conflict the figure in this card rises above any depression into the clear intoxicating air. In a way this card shows a background to the Nine. We become defensive and committed to fighting through an earlier experience of winning, staying on top. While the fight goes on we enjoy it. People under Wands' influence need to know they are alive, they need that charge of adrenalin to show them that the Fire still runs through them. Only later does the habit of constant battle close them in.

REVERSED

As implied in the picture the person is using the excitement of conflict to rise above uncertainty and depression. Reversed indicates sinking into anxiety, indecision, embarrassment. Right side up he was not so much in control of his life as staying on top of it. Here he can no longer put off the contradictions. Above all, the card warns against indecision, suggesting that if a person can come to a clear course of action the natural Wands self-confidence will return to overcome the anxieties and outer problems.

Figure 9

SIX

As the Wands progress down to the Ace they become stronger. The emphasis shifts from problems to joy, from defensiveness to optimism until, with the Ace, we become unified with the life-giving Fire. The Six marks a turning point. In the Golden Dawn system the card bears the title 'Victory', and we see, in fact, a victory parade, the hero crowned with a wreath and surrounded by his followers. However, he has not yet reached his destination. (A fiction, of course; he could just as easily be coming home. I am following Waite's lead on this.) He is assuming victory. Optimism produces the very success it desires and expects.

Often, though certainly not always, it requires only a true belief in ourselves to find the energy to accomplish what we want. More, such belief will inspire others to follow us. Sixes deal with communication and gifts. Here it is the Fire belief in life that Wands give to the people around them.

REVERSED
True optimism creates victory. False optimism, covering our doubts with bluster or illusion, leads to fear and weakness. The attitude shown in the card right side up cannot be faked, for when it does not work it becomes the opposite: defeatism, a sense that enemies will overwhelm us, or that life or specific people will betray us in some way. This attitude too often becomes a self-fulfilling prophecy, for suspicion can produce betrayal.

Figure 10

FIVE

Again conflict, but on a lighter level. It is in the nature of Wands to see life as battle, but in its best sense battle becomes an exciting struggle, eagerly sought after. The Fives in general show some difficulty or loss, but the element of Fire translates problems into competition, seen as a way in which people communicate with society and with each other. The young people are fighting, but not to hurt each other. Like children playing knights they bang their sticks together without really hitting anyone. They seek not to destroy but only to compete for the sheer joy of action.

REVERSED
The exciting competition right side up implies a sense of rules and fair play, for without understood agreements struggle as a game becomes impossible. Reversed, the card indicates that the rules are being abandoned, that in fact the battle has taken on a more serious, a nastier tone. The sense of play changes to bitterness or disillusionment as people seek actually to hurt or ruin each other. The Fire attitude to life, especially when not extended by Swords awareness and wisdom, demands that life respond in a positive way and not show its crueller side. The Five reversed brings to mind again that phrase 'the fire has gone out'.

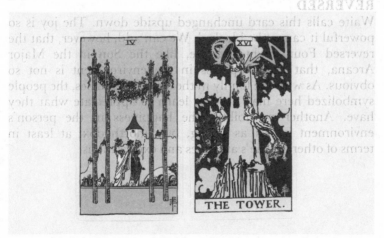

(a)   *Figure 11*   *(b)*

FOUR

The number four, with its image of the square, implies stasis or solidity. The irrepressible Wands energy, however, requires no protective fences as does, say, Pentacles. It will not be contained, and so we see people marching out ecstatically to the simplest of structures, trusting in the sun to burn off any clouds of trouble. The card represents a domestic environment filled with Fire optimism, eagerness, and celebration. As in the Six we see people following the dancers. Unlike that card, however, where the soldiers followed the charismatic leader, the people here are swept along by joy.

They are leaving a walled city for the open bower. In other words, their spirit and courage carry them from a defensive situation to an open one. We can contrast this image with that of the Tower, shown on the right. The two figures in that Major card are dressed very similarly (even to blue and red robes) to the two in the Four of Wands. In its less esoteric meanings the Tower shows the explosion that results when people allow a repressive or miserable situation to build up to an intolerable level. In the Four of Wands optimism and love of freedom carry the people, together, out of their walled city before it becomes a Tower-like prison.

REVERSED

Waite calls this card unchanged upside down. The joy is so powerful it cannot be blocked. We can add, however, that the reversed Four might indicate, like the Sun in the Major Arcana, that the happiness in the environment is not so obvious. As with the family in the Ten of Pentacles, the people symbolized here may need to learn to appreciate what they have. Another possibility: the happiness in the person's environment is just as strong, but unorthodox, at least in terms of other people's attitudes and expectations.

Figure 12

THREE

The number three, because it joins one and two in a new reality (see the Empress in the Major Arcana) indicates combinations and achievements. In each suit it shows that element in its maturity. With Wands this becomes accomplishment. The figure is shown strong, but at rest, unthreatened. The young competitors of Five have achieved success, especially in business, career, etc., though the card implies emotional maturity as well. The Wands eagerness does not vanish, but here he sends his ships out to explore new areas while he himself stays behind. In contrast to the Knight the image suggests keeping a solid basis in what we have already accomplished while we continue to open new areas and interests in ourselves. Sometimes in readings this can mean maintaining a primary commitment to existing relationships while still looking for new friends or lovers.

Some Tarot cards acquire special meanings that apply only to specific situations. For a person troubled or struggling with the past the Three of Wands can indicate becoming at peace with his or her memories. They become like boats sailing past on a wide river and then out to sea. The setting sun, a symbol of contentment, lights up the river, symbol of a person's emotional life, with a warm golden light.

In the Three of Wands we see the first of the Gate cards (the suit of Wands, with its emphasis on action, contains fewer of these inner cards than any of the other suits). Metaphysically the sea has always evoked in people a sense of the vastness and mystery of the universe, while rivers symbolize the experience of the ego dissolving into that great Sea. The boats represent that part of us which explores deep experience, while the man expresses the importance of rooting ourselves in ordinary reality before we attempt such metaphysical journeys. This schematic explanation gives only an intellectual shadow of the card's true meanings. That meaning lies in the experience of merging with the picture until the boats carry us into the unknown areas of the self. Significantly it is the addition of Water and Earth in the form of the sea and the rock which direct the images to Fire's greatest potential. Nevertheless, the special quality of this Gate, that of exploring the unknown, belongs to Fire.

REVERSED

Several meanings reflect the complex nature of the card right side up. On the one hand it can mean the failure of some 'exploration' or project (either practical or emotional) due to 'storms', that is, problems greater than we had hoped for or expected. But it can also mean becoming involved in our environment after a time of detachment and reflection. The image right side up carries a certain isolation as he looks down at the world. Finally, it can indicate being disturbed by memories.

Figure 13

TWO

Again a card of success, even greater than the Three, for here a man stands in a castle and holds the world in his hands. Yet the card does not carry the same contentment as the Three. He is bored; his accomplishments have only served to wall him in (a situation very unpleasant to Fire), and the world he holds is a very small one. Waite compares his weariness to that of Alexander, who supposedly wept after he had conquered the known world because he then could think of nothing else to do with his life (his death shortly afterwards no doubt gave this legend an extra boost).

Waite's comment suggests that the Wands love of battle and challenge can leave one with no real satisfaction in actual accomplishments when the fight has been won. Comparison with the Four (as well as the Ten) is obvious. There several people dance together, out from a walled city. Here one person stands alone, walled in by his own success.

REVERSED

Here we find one of Waite's best formulas: 'Surprise, wonder, enchantment, trouble, and fear'. All these terms together describe someone jumping directly into new experience. When we leave behind safe situations and past success to enter the unknown, we liberate so much emotion and energy that we cannot avoid either the wonder and enchantment or the fear that goes with it. The card speaks very strongly to people who have lived for a long time in some unpleasant or unsatisfying situation, and finally decide to make a change all at once.

Figure 14

ACE

A gift of strength, of power, of great sexual energy, of the love of living. The leaves burst out so abundantly that they fall off to become yods, the first letter of God's name. The yods' presence in all the Aces but that of Pentacles indicates that we receive these primal experiences as a gift from life. We cannot cause or produce them by any normal means; they come to us as hands emerging from clouds. Only by reaching the high states of awareness shown in the later cards of the Major Arcana can we understand the sources of these bursts of elemental energy. In ordinary situations it is enough to experience and appreciate them.

At the beginning of some situation, no card could signal a better start. It gives eagerness and strength. At the same time, the card teaches humility, for it reminds us that ultimately we have done nothing morally to deserve the optimism and greater energy that sometimes allows us to overwhelm other people.

REVERSED

A reversed Ace implies in some way a failure of that primal experience. This can mean simply that the situation turns against us, or, especially with Wands and Swords, that we find it impossible to hang on to that force and use it beneficially. Therefore, the Ace of Wands reversed can mean chaos, things falling apart, either because it just happened that way, or because we have ruined them through too much undirected energy. This can happen on a practical level, through too much activity, too many new starts without consolidating past gains; or emotionally, through being overconfident of friendship, or simply overbearing; or finally, sexually, through refusing to contain that fiery sexual appetite.

Waite included a much lighter reading for the reversed Ace: 'Clouded joy'. Then the Ace becomes like the Four or the Sun; the wonder and happiness exists even when we cannot, or will not, see it in front of us.

Chapter 2.

Cups

If Fire symbolizes the spirit force giving life to the universe, then Water signifies the love that allows the soul to receive that force. The sun draws the seed out of the ground, but only when water has first softened and nurtured it. Fire represents action, Water formlessness or passivity. Water does not symbolize weakness; rather it stands for the inner being, and that slow coming to life of the seed. In extreme situations water and fire are natural enemies; a flood will obliterate a fire, while a flame under a container will dissolve the already shapeless water into steam. At the same time life cannot exist or grow without a blending of these two primal opposites.

This paradox has led the alchemists and others to describe transformation – which is not simply change, but sudden evolution from a fragmented to an integrated state – as a unifying of Fire and Water, shown in the image of the her-maphrodite (in traditional society, with its strict identification of gender and role, what more powerful symbol of opposites existed than man and woman?), and more symbolically in the six-pointed star. In that ancient image (far older than its modern use as an emblem of Jewishness) the upward pointing Fire triangle joins the downward Water triangle to form a picture of life reaching out in all directions from a unified centre.

Because the water in a river changes constantly, yet the river always retains its basic character, rivers symbolize the true self that remains constant beneath all the outer changes in a person's life. Thus, while Fire symbolizes what we do, Water stands for what we are.

All rivers flow into the sea. However much our egos insist upon our separation from the rest of life, our instincts – the Water side of us – remind us of our harmony with the universe. Western culture has emphasized the idea of the individual as unique and separated from the world. The Tarot does not deny the individual's uniqueness – it insists on it, through the uniqueness of readings – but instead describes the individual as a combination of elements (an astrology chart, with its twelve signs and twelve houses, teaches the same lesson). And one of those elements remains a person's basic connection to the rest of life.

The suit of Cups shows an inner experience that flows rather than defines, that opens rather than restricts. Cups represent love and imagination, joy and peace, a sense of harmony and wonder. They show us love as the Way to Spirit, both the love we give to others and the love we receive from people and from life itself in its happier moments.

At times when life demands action, either physical or emotional, Cups represent the problem of passivity. All attempts to do anything, or to sort through some complicated problem, dissolve into vagueness, apathy, or empty dreams. Wands energize Cups, Swords define that emotional energy and give it direction, help it to figure things out (though an Air storm will agitate the peaceful Water), while Pentacles bring the fantasies back to the ground of real projects.

Figure 15

KING

Like the Kings of Wands, he represents his suit in terms of social responsibility, accomplishments and maturity. And like the Fire King, his position as 'maintainer of society' does not fit him all that comfortably. Cups symbolize the creative imagination, and to achieve success he has had to discipline and even suppress his dreams. The fish, symbol of creativity, hangs around his neck, but as an artificial ornament. He has directed his creative powers into socially responsible achievements. Waite describes him as a man of 'business, law, divinity'. In a sense he has matured his suit; but Water demands to flow, not to be confined.

Behind his throne a live fish jumps through the waves, signifying that creative imagination remains alive even when pushed to the background. Similarly, his throne floats on the lively sea, yet he himself does not touch the water (compare the Queen, p.52), indicating that his achievement derives ultimately from creativity, though he has shaped his life in such a way as to separate him from his own playful poet-like imagination.

In its extreme the imagery suggests someone who has dammed up his or her emotions and imagination. It also shows, more gently, a person who expresses these qualities, but not as central to her or his life. Responsibility comes before self-expression.

The King does not look at his cup; rather he holds it in the same way he holds his sceptre, symbol of power. Some commentators see the King as a person of troubled emotions, even anger and violence, who habitually suppresses these feelings even from himself, always maintaining a calm exterior. This interpretation derives from the idea that Kings stand for Air and therefore the King of Cups is Air of Water, the troubled emotions of Air covered by the benign influence of Water.

In some contexts, especially the arts, the King takes on a very different meaning. Because he is the leader of his suit, he can symbolize success, achievement, mastery, and maturity in artistic work.

REVERSED

More complex, and perhaps more troubled than the King of Wands, the King of Cups reversed slides towards dishonesty. When right side up he uses his creativity for his work; reversed, he turns his talents to vice or corruption. Swindlers also use creativity to further their careers, but we would not describe them as 'responsible'.

The card upside down can mean that the violent Air emotions emerge from their calm exterior, perhaps through the pressure of outside events. Romantically, the King of Cups reversed can suggest a dishonest yet domineering lover, more often male, sometimes female.

Finally, in relation to the arts, the King reversed can suggest that an artist's achievement has proved to be insignificant, or that a person has not yet matured and cannot point to a significant body of work. In a reading, this final meaning would come out strongly if the card appeared in connection with certain Pentacles reversed, such as the Eight, or the Three.

Figure 16

QUEEN

The most successful and balanced of the Cups, in some ways of all the Minor cards, the Queen is almost a mundane version of the World Dancer. Coming between the outer responsibility of the King and the passiveness of the Knight, she shows the possibility of blending imagination and action, creativity and social usefulness. Her throne, decorated with cherubic mermaids, sits on land, indicating her vital connection to the outer world and to other people, a connection more real than the King's. At the same time the water flows over her feet and merges with her dress, signifying the unity of self with emotion and imagination. The water suggests also unconscious forces – the underlying spiritual patterns shown in the Major Arcana – nourishing conscious life. The unity of water, land, and the Queen implies that we do not feed the imagination by giving it complete freedom to wander where it will, but rather by directing it into valuable activity, an idea that most artists would endorse. This idea appears even more strongly in the Nine of Pentacles, emblem of creative discipline.

Waite describes the cup she holds as her own creation. It is the most elaborate of the Cups (whatever we may think about its style!) and symbolizes the achievement brought about through using the imagination. Notice its church-like shape. Until the modern age (and still in more archaic cultures) all art expressed and glorified spiritual experience. The Queen stares at the cup intently, showing the strong will that directs and moulds creative force without suppressing it. At the same time her look suggests that the creative person derives inspiration for future activity from her or his past achievements. Compare her fierce gaze with the dreaminess of the Knight, or the cloudy fantasies of the Seven.

Will power alone will not unite imagination and action. Only love can give meaning to her actions, and realize her goals. These goals are not simply creative in the narrow sense of art, but in the wider sense of making something whole and alive out of the opportunities and elements given by life. They can include emotional goals, especially family, for while the King symbolizes society, the Queen symbolizes the family, for men as well as women.

What is most important is that she joins consciousness to feeling. She knows what she wants and will take the steps necessary to get it. Yet she acts always with an awareness of love.

Waite says 'loving intelligence and hence the gift of vision', terms suggesting that a vision of life as joyful can only come as a gift, but love can open us to receiving such a gift, to recognizing that it exists. With intelligence joined to love we return the gift by taking that vision and making something real and lasting from it.

REVERSED
Reversing the Queen of Cups breaks that unity of vision and action. We see someone ambitious and powerful, yet dangerous, because she cannot be trusted. The love has become lost, and with it the commitment to values greater than her own success. If she slides further from the balance, she can become dishonourable, even depraved, as her creative force lurches out of control.

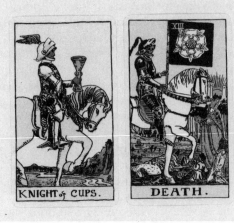

(a)   *Figure 17*   *(b)*

KNIGHT

As a less developed figure than the Queen or King, he has not learned to direct his imagination into the world. Therefore dreams dominate this card, with its images of a slow horse, and a knight lost in the enticements of his cup, symbol of the imagination. At the same time the creative force is less powerful here than in any of the other Cups court cards. Only a narrow river flows through a parched land. The Knight has not learned that the true imagination feeds on action rather than fantasy. By this I mean that if we do nothing with our dreams they remain vague and unrelated to the rest of our lives.

We may make another point about the Knight's dreaminess. What feeds it – inner principles, as in myth or archetypal art; or self-indulgence, as in daydreams and escapist films or books? The English poet, Samuel Taylor Coleridge, distinguished between 'imagination' and 'fancy'. Both take the mind away from ordinary experience and perceptions. However, while the first derives from and leads to an awareness of underlying spiritual truth, the second produces only fantasies that may excite, but ultimately lack real meaning. They derive from the ego rather than the unconscious.

Nothing emerges from his cup (compare the Page; p.56).

Nor has he shaped it into something greater than it was, as has the Queen. A Knight is a figure committed to action and involvement. Water, on the other hand, symbolizes passiveness. The symbolism – Fire of Water in the Golden Dawn system – indicates the elements as unreconciled. By denying this basic commitment to the world, he does not allow his imagination to produce anything.

Because he is a Knight the outside world of action, of sex, may pull him even while he pursues his thoughts and fantasies. His passiveness can sometimes be a pose, almost exaggerated for the purpose of denying those temptations and desires which disturb his peace. Romantically the Knight can represent a lover who does not wish to commit him or herself, who is perhaps attractive yet passive, withdrawn, or narcissistic.

These harsh images of the Knight all deal with his conflicts. At the same time his helmet and feet are winged, his horse is spirited in its slowness. And he resembles Death, symbol of transformation. If the Knight is not pulled by responsibility or desire, if he follows a genuine vision rather than escape from outside commitments, then he can go very deeply into himself, turning the Knight energy into an exploration of his own inner world.

REVERSED

In various ways we see the Knight reacting towards increased demands from the world beyond himself. It can mean simply that he rouses himself to action or else follows his more physical desires. Or it can mean that a passive person is being pushed towards action or commitment and does not like it. Without outwardly resisting he or she can resent those demands. The result can be a wall built up between the Knight and those people who are making him act out his responsibilities. This attitude can result in hypocrisy or manipulation, sometimes lies and tricks.

Figure 18

PAGE

Being younger in spirit, child-like, the Page does not suffer the same conflict with either responsibility or sensual desire. He indicates a state or a time in which contemplation and fantasy are very proper to a person. No outside demands disturb his or her gentle contemplation. As a result the fish of imagination looks at him from his cup. Amused, he looks back at it without the Knight's need to penetrate so deeply into himself. Here, the imagination is its own justification.

The fish can also symbolize psychic talents and sensitivity. And since the Pages all have a student quality, the Page of Cups can show someone developing psychic abilities, either through an actual programme of study and/or meditation, or else such talents developing by themselves, but in a peaceful way.

REVERSED

Right side up we saw a person letting his imagination bubble up before him. Because he does nothing with his fantasies they give him no trouble. If he acts upon them, however, they may lead him into mistakes. Reversed therefore means to follow our inclinations, to act without thinking, or to allow our immediate desires to seduce us, particularly if they go against our common sense. We see the reversed Page whenever we buy something we do not need and do not even really want; we see him when we make promises we cannot keep or commitments that do not really mean anything.

In other situations, if the Page refers to psychic development, or true visions, then reversed shows a person disturbed by these visions. For many people in our rationalized world the sudden emergence of psychic talent, even if deliberately sought through training, can appear very frightening. The reversed Page mirrors the fear and reminds us to calm down, to look peacefully at the fish rising from the cup of ourselves. In connection with Pentacles it calls for grounding in outer reality to avoid being washed away by fantasies or visions.

Figure 19

TEN

As the highest number, the Tens signify being filled with the quality of the suit. In Wands we saw an excess of burdens; in Cups we find joy and the wonder of life spread across the sky. The holy Grail, symbol of God's grace and love, rests at the base of this suit, showing us that love, imagination, and joy all come to us as gifts. The Bible tells us that God made the rainbow as a promise that the world will never again suffer a flood of destruction. But the rainbow carries a more positive promise as well – that life brings happiness and not just an absence of pain.

The man and woman in the picture understand these things. Arm in arm they look up and celebrate the rainbow. The children, however, dance without looking up. They symbolize innocence, which takes happiness as the natural condition of life. They expect happiness, but do not waste it. Showing a family, the card refers primarily to domestic happiness, but can indicate any situation that brings a surge of joy. It especially refers to the recognition of the valuable qualities in a situation. This meaning pertains especially in readings where the Ten of Cups appears in contrast to the Ten of Pentacles.

REVERSED

There are two basic variants here. First, all the emotion turns against itself. Some highly-charged situation, usually romantic or domestic, has gone wrong, producing violent feeling, anger, or deceit. Or, in practice, the reversed Ten can simply mean that a person does not recognize or appreciate the happiness life is offering him or her.

Figure 20

NINE

From deep joy we move to the simpler pleasures of feasting and physical contentment. As noted earlier, the Nines depict the compromises we make with life. Wands showed a strong

defence; the more benign Cups demonstrate the attitude of
avoiding worry and problems by concentrating on ordinary
pleasures. People sometimes react antagonistically to this
card, perhaps wishing to see themselves as beyond super-
ficiality. At times, especially after troubles or a period of long,
hard work, nothing can serve us better than a simple good
time.

REVERSED
For once the reversed meaning gives the greater awareness –
to use Waite's formula, 'truth, loyalty, liberty'. In connection
with the right side up meaning, the words imply a rejection of
surface values; but they also refer to very tangled or oppressive
situations where, by clinging to the thread of truth, or by
staying loyal to ourselves, or to others, or to a purpose, we can
bring about victory and liberation.

(a)   Figure 21   (b)

EIGHT

The pleasant nature of Cups tends to lull us away from what
we have to do. The Eight begins (or ends) a series of five cards
dealing with the Water problem of action. In this card we see
someone turning his back on a double row of standing Cups
which symbolize a situation that not only has provided
happiness, but actually continues to do so. In contrast to the

Five, all the Cups remain upright; nothing has been knocked over. And yet the person knows that the time has come to leave. The imagery suggests one of the true uses of Water instinct – an ability to sense when something has ended before it either dries up or comes crashing down around us, to know the time to move on.

We see the figure climbing a hill, going to higher ground, with the implication of moving from a less to a more meaningful situation. Notice the resemblance of the figure to the Hermit beside him. To reach the height of the Hermit's wisdom, we must first put the ordinary things of life behind us.

The Hermit reminds us that the image of land does not necessarily mean action or involvement in the ordinary sense, but can suggest almost the opposite: that is, withdrawing from outer activity to seek a greater self-awareness. At first the scene appears to take place at night; but when we look closer we see that actually it depicts an eclipse, with the moon moving across the sun. A moon phase, that is, a period of inner awareness, has taken over from outer-directed activity. By joining moon imagery to a scene of movement, the card teaches us that developing a deeper sense of self is also an action. Remember that the Hermit, by reversing the sexual polarity of the High Priestess above him, combines action and intuition in a definite programme of self-knowledge.

Whether we view the figure as moving away from the world, or into action, the card symbolizes leaving a stable situation. In its deepest level this card acts as a Gate, similar in certain ways to the Three of Wands. Both work through the image of a journey into the unknown, but while the Fire card is drawn to Water, the Water card is drawn to Air. The Three of Wands breaks down the ego and frees the exploring spirit, while the Eight of Cups moves from the vagueness of Water to the specific knowledge of abstract principles symbolized by the climb up the Hermit's mountain.

REVERSED
Sometimes the upside down Eight indicates the simple negation of the card's basic image – a refusal to leave some situation, a determination to hang on even when we know deep inside that we have taken all we can from it. Such a description characterizes many relationships.

Usually, however, the card reversed maintains its quality of awareness and correct response. It symbolizes that the time to leave has *not* come, that the situation will continue to give joy and meaning.

One final possibility: timidity, leaving a situation because a person lacks the courage to pursue it and take everything she or he can get from it. Many people make this a pattern in their lives; they become involved in relationships, work, projects, etc., and then run away, either when difficulties arise, or when the time comes for genuine commitment.

Figure 22

SEVEN

With the Seven, the Cups problem emerges in its most direct form. Emotion and imagination can produce wonderful visions, but without a grounding in both action and the outer realities of life these fantastic images remain daydreams, 'fancies' without real meaning or value. Notice that the visions cover the whole range of fantasies from wealth (the jewels), to a victory wreath, to fear (the dragon), to adventure (the castle), even the archetypes of mythology — a godlike face, a mysterious radiant figure, and a snake, universal symbol of psychic wisdom. It is a mistake to think that daydreams are meaningless because of their *content*; on the contrary they often spring from deep archetypal needs and images. They lack meaning because they do not connect to anything outside themselves.

REVERSED
This card reversed means a determination to make something from dreams. This does not mean rejecting fantasies, but rather doing something with them.

Figure 23

SIX

As cards of benevolent emotion and dreams the Cups signify sweet memories. Sometimes these memories truly represent the past; at other times we may idealize the past and see it through a haze of security and happiness. The emblem of this second attitude is childhood, pictured as a safe time, when parents, or older brothers and sisters, protected us and gave us everything we needed. Sometimes such an attitude can produce a warm secure feeling which will help people face their current problems. In this sense the card shows the past (the dwarf) giving a gift of memories to the future, symbolized by the child. At other times, however, a fixation on the past can prevent a person from facing current problems. The past can distract from the present just as much as fantasies of the future.

There are other meanings for the Six beside memory. The

Sixes show relationships of giving and receiving. Here we see
the image of a teacher or protector giving wisdom and security
to someone who might be a family member, a student, or a
friend.

REVERSED
Like the Seven, the Six reversed indicates a move towards
action. Specifically, it shows looking towards the future,
rather than the past. The two cards reversed are very similar;
the difference is that the Six shows an attitude while the Seven
indicates actual steps taken.

At other times, depending on the right side up meaning, the
Six reversed indicates disturbed memories (compare the
Three of Wands reversed), or a feeling of alienation from the
past. It can also show the breakdown of a relationship based
on one person protecting or teaching the other(s).

Figure 24

FIVE

The Fives concern struggle and sometimes pain. With Wands
we saw the adventure of competition; Cups show the
emotional reaction to loss. The picture depicts sorrow but also
acceptance. Three cups lie spilled out, but two remain
standing, even if at the moment the figure concentrates on the
three. In readings I have often seen this card linked to either

the Three of Cups as a happiness or hope that has failed, or
else the Three of Swords; the two cups standing have often
referred to the Two of Cups, that is, support from a lover or
friend.

The woman (or man; the androgynous character of the
figure indicates that sorrow unites the sexes) stands rigid,
wrapped in black, the colour of grief. She needs to accept that
some happiness has suddenly vanished, been knocked over.
She does not yet realize that something remains, for first she
must understand and accept the loss. Has she herself knocked
over the cups, either through recklessness or by taking them
for granted? In the sense of awareness the card relates to
Justice, emblem of truth and the acceptance of responsibility.
In her pose and costume she resembles the Hermit, who
cloaks himself in wisdom to hold him upright in his task of
looking within for a vision of his life, the vision he will accept
in Justice.

The river represents the flow of sorrow but the bridge symbolizes consciousness and determination. It leads from the
past (loss) to the future (new beginnings). When she has
accepted her loss she can then turn, pick up the two remaining
cups, and cross over the bridge to the house, symbol of
stability and continuity.

With its deep evocation of regret the card forms another
Gate, bringing to us that sense of spiritual loss and separation
which all over the world has given rise to myths of a fall or an
exile from Paradise.

REVERSED
The basic meaning of the card can change in three ways when
reversed. First, it can mean not accepting the loss, and as an
extension of this, false projects or mistakes. Second, it can
indicate support from others, friendship, new interests and
occupations after some sad or disturbing event. Finally, it can
emphasize an awareness of what remains important and permanent in the face of sorrow. In this sense the woman turns
from the three to the two. Here the two cups symbolize the
solid basis of a person's life; they remain standing because
they are not so easily knocked over. And this awareness
indicates that the three fallen cups symbolize something less
important than might at first seem at the time of its destruction.

Figure 25

FOUR

The passiveness of Cups can sometimes lead to apathy. What we can call the 'negative imagination' makes us look at everything as worthless or boring. There seems to be nothing worth getting up for, nothing worth doing, and nothing worth examining.

The three cups symbolize the person's past experience. Bored by what life has given him he does not recognize the new opportunities being offered to him by the fourth cup. The resemblance of that cup to the Ace suggests that the new possibilities can lead to happiness and satisfaction. In the main, however, the card shows a situation when everything in life has come to appear the same. The card sometimes shows apathy resulting from a dull, unstimulating environment.

REVERSED

Again, the reversal takes us out of ourselves and awakens us to the world and its possibilities. New things are offered, new relations, new ideas. Most important, the reversed card shows enthusiasm and the seizing of opportunities.

Figure 26

THREE

The Threes show an appreciation of the meaning and value of the suit. Because of the Grail at the base of the suit, the Three of Cups indicates joy, celebration, and above all sharing the wonder of life. As if we had passed the crisis of action, the final three cards all, according to their numbers, flow with happiness. Here we see the women celebrating, as at a harvest. Either a crisis has finished, or work has produced good results.

We see the three women so intertwined we can hardly tell whose arm is whose. In bad times as well as good, the card shows a sharing of experience.

REVERSED
Again several meanings present themselves. First of all it can show the loss of some happiness. Very often it indicates that something hoped for has not come about. It can also signify the failure of friendship, and again the disillusionment of finding that friends have not supported us when we needed them, or else the break up of a group of friends.

Another meaning shows a corruption of the original. Rather than a shared celebration of life's joys we find what Waite quaintly calls 'excess in physical enjoyment and the pleasures of the senses'. Obviously Waite intended this to mean that deeper values are ignored. It is worth observing, however, that most people find this phrase, especially as a prediction, not at all unpleasant.

(a) (b) (c)

Figure 27

TWO

In many ways this card acts as a lesser version of the Lovers. While the trump shows the great power of mature sexual relationships the Minor card emphasizes the beginning of a relationship. This is not a hard and fast rule as far as readings are concerned. The Two can often show a long-term union or friendship, perhaps on a lighter level than the Lovers. In study, and most commonly in practice, however, it indicates the pledging of friendship, the beginning of a love affair.

In the trump we see the Angel, symbol of super-con-sciousness. In the Two of Cups we see the winged lion over the caduceus of Hermes, symbol of healing and wisdom. In both cases, the card shows how two people by uniting their separate qualities and abilities through love, produce some-thing in their lives beyond what either would have achieved alone. The lion symbolizes sexuality, the wings Spirit. Love gives a greater meaning to the sexual drive that leads us to it.

In Part One of this book we saw how the Lovers can serve as a diagram of the unified self. We can look at the Two of Cups in a similar way. While the man symbolizes action and movement, the woman symbolizes emotion, sensitivity, and an appreciation of experience. By uniting these two qualities we give our lives value.

Notice the resemblance of the man to the Fool. In a reading these two cards came up linked together. The woman, an artist, wanted to know what direction her work should take. She was especially concerned to investigate whether her art came from a real centre in her life or was simply an intellectual exercise. Now, other cards indicated she had reached a level of technical mastery in what she had been doing, while the Fool, as an outcome, showed her taking a leap into a new area. But the Two of Cups showed she would find success if she linked her technical ability and explorations to the spiritual grounding symbolized by the woman.

REVERSED
In different ways the reversed card shows a breakdown of the ideals symbolized right side up. It can mean a love affair or friendship which has gone sour in some way, in particular because of jealousy and a breakdown of trust. It can mean simply the end of a relationship. Depending on the cards around it, it can signify a relationship endangered by internal or external pressures. Another possibility is infatuation, when people pretend to others, to themselves, that a love affair means more than it actually does. In a similar vein the reversed card can show people going through the motions of a love affair, with one or both of them not really caring.

If we look at the card as signifying the self, then reversed indicates a split between what we do and what we feel, between action and emotion.

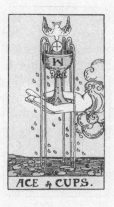

Figure 28

ACE

From the King's conflicting emotions, through the various balances of celebration and passivity, we arrive finally at the Ace – emblem of love underpinning life. The Ace of Cups has the immediate meaning of a time of happiness and love, a gift of joy. Just as fire makes the world, so love gives it value.

The Smith picture, with its dove and wafer, specifically shows the Holy Grail, said to contain the physical presence of the Holy Ghost at work in the world. In the more subtle versions of the King Arthur legend, it was not really chivalry – that is, a moral structure – that held together King Arthur's glorious kingdom, but rather the secret presence of the Holy Grail hidden in the land. When the Grail left (because Arthur's knights failed to approach it in a spiritual way) the kingdom fell apart. The allegory tells us that the world does not function primarily by its laws, its moral order and its social structures, but rather by the spiritual basis which gives all these things meaning, and protects them from corruption. When we look at existence as something solely to be conquered (the way Arthur's knights went after the Grail) we bring only chaos. Cups – Water – symbolize receptivity. Love, and ultimately life, cannot be seized, but only accepted.

REVERSED

The reversed Ace always brings disruption. Here we see unhappiness, violence, destruction – the very conditions acted out in the King Arthur legend when the Grail had left the kingdom. The reversed card can indicate simply that the times have turned against us and we can only accept that life brings problems as well as joy. Or, the card upside down can imply that we ourselves bring about our unhappiness by not recognizing what life offers us, or by reacting violently when what we need is calm.

Chapter 3.
Swords

KNIGHT of SWORDS.

In many ways Swords are the most difficult suit. The very object, a weapon, signifies pain, anger, destruction, and it is mostly these experiences that the Swords image depict. Yet a sword can also symbolize cutting through illusions and complicated problems (remember Alexander cutting through the Gordian knot). Galahad, the knight who achieved the Holy Grail, could not begin his spiritual quest until he had received his magic sword from Merlin, the kingdom's guide. Similarly, we cannot begin our own quests for meaning and value in life until we have learned to recognize and accept the truth, whatever pain it brings.

Swords belong to the element of Air, or wind, often seen as the closest to Ether, or Spirit. The word 'spirit' relates directly to the word 'breath', and in Hebrew the word for 'spirit' and the word for 'wind' are the same. Just as air constantly moves, so the mind never rests, twisting and turning, sometimes violent, sometimes calm, but always moving. Anyone who has tried to meditate will know how persistently the mind moves.

One problem connected with Swords is that of 'ungrounded thought' or what we might call a 'Hamlet complex'. The mind sees so many sides to a situation, so many possibilities, that understanding, let alone action, becomes impossible. Because our culture has always emphasized rationality, many people today see thinking in general as the cause of all life's problems. If we just stop thinking, they tell us, then everything will work out all right. Even if such a thing were possible, the Tarot tells us it would not benefit us. We do not overcome the problem of an element by banishing it or replacing it with something, but rather by combining it with other elements. The fact is, the more confused we are the more we need our minds, because nothing else can sort out the truth. We need also, however, to combine Air with Water – that is, emotion with receptivity. We need also to combine it with Ether, Spirit, the deep values grounded in spiritual/psychological truth that we see embodied in the Major Arcana. Then the problem of Air changes to the Way, wisdom.

The more obvious problem shown in Swords is that of sorrow, pain, anger – the stormy side of Air. We cannot overcome these things by ignoring them, but we can add to Swords the optimism of Wands, and we can use Pentacles to take ourselves out of our emotions through an involvement with work, nature, the outside world.

(a)   (b)   (c)

Figure 29

KING

As a maintainer of the social structure the King represents
authority, power, and judgement. He takes the mental energy
of Air and uses it to uphold and rule the world with the
keenness of his mind and the force of his personality. His
crown is yellow, the colour of mental energy, while his mantle
is purple, for wisdom. His cap, a burnouse-like head-dress, is
red, the colour of action. The King's intellect does not exist for
itself alone, but rather for what it can *do*, as a tool of authority.
Similarly, his sword, unlike that of the Queen of Swords or of
Justice, does not point straight up, for pure wisdom, but
rather tilts slightly to the right, the side of action. The require-
ment to act upon his judgements tends to distort the power of

judgement itself, a fact we can see if we compare the situation of an academic observer of politics with that of someone running a country.

Moreover, the emphasis on social-minded 'realism' may narrow his viewpoint to a very limited materialism. We can see him in the man or woman priding him or herself on tough-minded common sense, with no time for 'mystic mumbo jumbo'. Such people usually ignore how much of their thinking depends on preconception and prejudice, rather than observation of life.

Notice the resemblance to the Emperor. We can call the King the Emperor's representative in the real world. While the trump embodies the archetype of order, law, society, the King of Swords maintains these principles in practice.

Two birds, the animal emblem of the Swords court cards, fly behind the throne. The bird symbolizes the mind's ability to take us into the high air of wisdom, removed from fiery passion, watery emotion, or earthly material corruption. The number two, on the other hand, symbolizes choice, the constant tension between abstract thought and the action that must be taken in the world.

But if the birds symbolize the mind's ability to climb above the world they also symbolize the remoteness such an attitude can produce. Notice, that the King's throne is seemingly in the clouds. Like the King of Wands, the Swords King can tend towards arrogance, his powerful mind and will setting him above the more confused people around him. In social terms the imagery suggests the tendency of government and rulers to divorce their judgements from the real needs of people. In more personal terms, we see the remote King in men or women who are harsh, cold, judgemental. As a husband or lover, the King of Swords often indicates a domineering or controlling person.

In his best sense the King of Swords evokes Justice, the card directly beneath the Emperor in the Major Arcana. When he connects with this trump, the King stands for social justice, wise laws, and above all, a commitment to intellectual honesty, and the need to put knowledge into practice. Like Justice, and alone of all the court cards, he stares directly out at us, a master of wisdom compelling us to recognize and hold to the truth.

REVERSED

Right side up the King walks a narrow line between committed intellect and power for its own sake. Reversed, he tends to fall on the wrong side of that line. He is authority corrupted, strength used for its own ends of power and dominance.

In readings, we must always take such strong imagery into consideration. The reversed King (or any reversed court card) may simply mean some person in difficulty. In connection with the Queen or the Knight it may mean a difficult relationship or a failure to mature (see the section on Readings for relationships between court cards of the same suit). By itself, however, it symbolizes the arrogance of a powerful mind turned in on itself, recognizing only its own desire for control.

Figure 30

QUEEN

As the yin aspect of the suit, the Queen of Swords symbolizes experiences of both sorrow and wisdom, and especially the connection between them. Having experienced pain (the card sometimes signifies widowhood), and having faced it with courage, acceptance, and honesty, she has found wisdom.

The tassel hanging from her left wrist (the side of experience) resembles a cut rope (compare the Eight of Swords, p.82). She has used the sword of her intellect to free herself from confusion, doubt, and fear; now, although she frowns at the world, she opens her hand to it. Though clouds gather around her, her head remains above them in the clear air of truth. One bird, a symbol of the purity of her wisdom, flies high above her. Her sword, like that of Justice and the Ace, stands straight up.

In the sense that powerless women will often suffer from the actions of men, the card refers specifically to women. In its character, it can represent someone of either sex, for neither sorrow nor courage are restricted by gender.

REVERSED

The reversed Queen can indicate an overemphasis on sorrow, someone who makes life seem much worse than it is by ignoring the good things around her. She can also show a strong mind turned nasty, especially as a reaction to pain or pressure from unpleasant situations or people. Sometimes she represents a person so forceful she or he expects, not just demands, that everyone around her, even life itself, will do what she wants.

When people oppose her, the Queen turns malicious, narrow minded, bigoted, and like the King, uses her attitudes to force her personality on the people around her. Whether she represents an excess of sorrow or egoism, she has lost the right side up commitment to truth.

Figure 31

KNIGHT

The young Knight, whose youth makes him both freer of social responsibility than the King, and less tempered by experience than the Queen, rides directly into the storm, waving his sword in his eagerness to overcome all difficulties. He is brave, skilful, strong; yet he tends also towards wildness, even fanatacism. He recognizes no limits.

And yet he often does not know how to sustain a long struggle. He expects his enemies and life's problems to fall under his charge and cannot so easily handle a situation that requires long, steady plodding.

His eagerness suggests a certain innocence, like a young knight who has never lost a battle. His bravery, his skill, his readiness to charge all problems, can sometimes contain a fear of losing that innocence, that strong belief in himself. For he knows inside that he has yet to face and overcome life's greater difficulties. The opposite in many ways of the Knight of Cups, he directs all his energy outwards; he is perhaps nervous of being quietly alone with himself.

REVERSED

As with the King and Queen his weaknesses take over. He is extravagant, careless, excessive. His charge becomes wild, a mistaken response to a situation that calls for a quieter more careful approach.

Figure 32

PAGE

A much lighter card than the other court Swords, the Page represents a very different approach to problems than the Knight (notice that while the King and Queen emphasize wisdom, the two 'younger' cards deal with Swords' more immediate quality of conflict). Rather than charge them he finds it sufficient to simply get above them, to find the high ground. Instead of solving conflicts or meeting opposition he detaches himself.

If the situation is one that calls for such an easygoing approach then the Page's unattached attitude is very beneficial. But if a more difficult problem is involved, then the Page's practice becomes hard to maintain. It requires 'vigilance' to use Waite's term, making sure that people or situations do not get too close. Much of the Page's energy goes to looking over his shoulder. As a somewhat aged student, Hamlet embodied the Page's attitude of observation and irony. His situation, however, called for the aggressive approach of the Knight.

Because of his detached quality the Page can sometimes indulge himself in spying on people, either literally, or figuratively, as an attitude to life. In other words, he may look on human life as a kind of curious spectacle in which he himself does not expect to take part.

REVERSED

Here we see the effect of the Page's aloof attitude in a situation that requires more force. The vigilance turns to paranoia; everyone appears to be an enemy. What began as a feeling of 'I'm above all that, I don't need to concern myself with that,' becomes an obsession with problems and a seeming inability to do anything about them. Such feelings of weakness are endemic to Swords; they require Wands for courage and optimism.

Figure 33

TEN

From the blue skies of the court cards to the black gloom of the Ten and Nine. Just as the Ten of Cups showed joy overflowing, so the Ten of Swords fills us with pain. Despite the extreme picture the card does not represent death, or even especially violence. It signifies more of a reaction to problems than the problems themselves.

It takes only one sword to kill someone. The ten swords in the man's body, even including one in his ear, suggest hysteria, and the adolescent attitude that 'no one has ever suffered so much as me', 'my life is over', and so on. Notice that in contrast to the Nine the sky clears in the distance, the black clouds give way to sunshine, and that in contrast to the Five or the Two, the water lies placidly. The situation is not so bad as it looks.

REVERSED

Turn this card round and we can imagine the swords falling out of his back. Waite describes it as success and advantage, but not permanent. These ideas suggest that when a situation changes, the problems may go away for the moment. However, the person must now take advantage of this relief by making a real change in her or his condition – either practical or mental, depending on the need – so that the situation will not revert to what it was. The card bears a relationship to the Ten of Wands reversed, where we saw the danger of picking up the sticks again once the situation has calmed down.

Figure 34

NINE

The image of deepest sorrow, of utmost mental pain. Where the Queen frees herself by turning sorrow into wisdom, and the Three suggests the calm of acceptance, the Nine shows the moment of agony, of dissolution. The Swords do not stick in her back, but hang in the black air above her. Very often the Nine refers not to something happening directly to us, but rather to someone we love.

Love, in fact, fills the card and gives it its meaning. The blanket design shows roses, symbol of passion, alternating with the signs of the zodiac. In the card's deepest sense it shows a mind that takes on itself all the sorrows of the world, the Lamed Vav, or Just Man, of Jewish legend.

Can we see a way out of such dreadful pain? Both Buddha and Christ pictured the world as a place of unending sorrow, yet both also said that tragedy remains always a half truth, that the universe seen as a whole brings joy and peace. And Nietzsche wrote of embracing existence so completely, with such total ecstatic honesty, that we would gladly repeat, endlessly, every moment of our lives, whatever the pain.

REVERSED

For the Nine reversed Waite gives one of his most suggestive formulas: 'Imprisonment, suspicion, doubt, reasonable fear, and shame'. The words delineate a state of mind or rather a progression of states that result when people retreat into themselves from some problem they do not dare to confront.

As with the card right side up, the reversed card deals with our reaction to something outside ourselves, but here it is oppression rather than tragedy. The key term is 'reasonable fear', which can refer to, say, political oppression – as of racial or sexual minorities; or social oppression – a feeling of being a scapegoat because of appearance, speech, etc.; or simply the personal oppression of a domineering family or partner. The important thing is that the problem is real, but because we cannot directly attack it, we tend to hide in ourselves, keeping in our anger and resentment.

Anger turned in on itself becomes depression and from there suspicion. The person who was laughed at as a child for her big nose thinks that everyone is looking at her. The black person believes that any complaint at work is a racial slur. And suspicion easily leads to self-doubt and shame. Often it does not even help, at least not completely, if we rationally know that we have no reason to feel ashamed, that in fact those who have ridiculed or oppressed us should feel the shame. Unless the oppressed self-doubting person takes action, expresses her or his anger, makes real changes in her or his life, the deep hidden shame will remain.

Figure 35

EIGHT

From the Nine reversed we move to an even clearer image of oppression. We see a person tied up, surrounded by swords with a castle – symbol of authority – behind her; she stands in the mud, an image of humiliation and shame. Notice, however, that the swords do not actually fence her in, and the ropes do not go around her legs, while the people who have tied her up do not appear at all in the card. In short, nothing prevents her from just leaving.

The clue to this card is the blindfold – symbolizing confusion, oppressive ideas, isolation from other people in similar situations; what political liberationists call 'mystification' – keeping people down not by direct force, but by training them to believe in their own helplessness. In that remarkable way the Tarot has of summing up a complex situation the card can almost stand as a diagram of the oppressed condition.

On a very different level the Eight of Swords acts as a Gate to a special awareness. By identifying with it we gain a sense of our own ignorant condition, something which many people will intellectually recognise (paradox of paradoxes) but not really accept. Without enlightenment, or what some Sufis and others call 'conscious evolution', we can never really know ourselves or the world, can never say 'This is the truth; this is the way things really are'. Recognition of ignorance is the first (and often the hardest) step to true knowledge.

REVERSED
Freedom begins when we throw off our blindfolds, when we see clearly how we have arrived in whatever situation we are in, what we have done, what others have done (particularly those who have bound us, but also others in similar situations), and what we can do about it now. The reversed Eight means, in general, liberation from some oppressive situation; primarily it refers to the first step of such liberation, that is, seeing things as clearly as possible.

Figure 36

SEVEN

The theme of struggle continues. Here we see an image of taking action against problems. Sometimes the card means simply a daring act, even a coup that takes the sting out of opposition. More often, it stands for an impulsive act when a careful plan is required.

The picture shows us someone grinning as he makes off with his enemy's weapons. He has not attacked the camp, he cannot even carry all the swords. The card implies schemes and actions that do not solve anything. Not as obvious, but sometimes more important, is the sense of isolation involved. He is acting alone, unable or unwilling to get anyone's help.

Going a step further, this card can indicate craftiness, but with the flaw of habitually hiding, often for no real reason, one's true plans or intentions.

REVERSED

The isolation turns around to become communication, in particular seeking advice on what to do about one's problems. Valuable as the specific instructions can be, just as important is the person's readiness to listen and to seek help. The card can sometimes refer to the *act* of finding help, such as consulting a reader or a therapist or simply friends.

Like all else the value of the image depends on context. Where self-reliance is required the Seven of Swords reversed can imply an overdependence on others telling us what to do. When the card reversed appears in opposition to the Fool or the Hanged Man, we must look to the other cards to determine which course – independence or seeking advice — will produce the best results.

Figure 37

SIX

A strange and powerful image, this card more than any other illustrates how Pamela Smith's images reach beyond Arthur Waite's formulas. *The Pictorial Key* says 'journey by water, route, way, expedient'. But the picture of a ferryboat at twilight, carrying shrouded figures to a wooded isle, suggests a more spiritual journey – in myth, Charon carrying the dead across the River Styx. A great silence fills this card, like the silence of Salvador Dali's paintings.

Usually this card does not signify death, though it can indicate mourning; nor does it show transformation, in the sense of Death in the Major Arcana. Rather it depicts a quiet passage through a difficult time. Waite says, 'The freight is light'; and Eden Gray writes, 'The swords do not weigh down the boat'. Though we carry our troubles with us we have adapted to them; they will not sink us or bear us down. On a simple level it means functioning in some difficult situation without attacking the problems. It can refer to an immedaite problem or a situation that has gone on for years. Looking deeper we see the image of a long sorrow – mourning is an example, but not the only one – which a person has felt for so long that it no longer gives pain, but has become part of life.

There is another, less disturbing meaning – that of a quiet passage, physically (certainly the literal meaning of a journey must not be forgotten) or spiritually, a time of easy transition. Notice the ferryman's black pole. Black indicates potentiality; where nothing final has happened, all things remain possible. By staying calm we waste neither energy nor opportunity.

The Six of Swords is a Gate. Looking at it with sensitivity and then entering the picture will produce first a quieting effect on the mind and then later, slowly, a sense of movement within the self.

REVERSED
Seen in one way the balance and peace become disturbed; the passage is no longer serene for the water, symbol of emotion, becomes stirred up. So the reversed card can suggest a stormy journey, physically or spiritually. It can refer also to the idea that when we try to attack some longstanding problem, especially one accepted by everyone else, we agitate the situation. As one example, an unsatisfying or oppressive relationship can go quietly along for years until one of the members decides to do something about it. To try to remove the swords from the boat can sink it, for the swords, after all, are plugging up the holes.

In another way, the Six reversed can show communication, reminding us that right side up the people maintain their composure by not speaking or looking at each other. If the swords symbolize unhappy memories and the silence is a defence then communication can be painful. It can also begin healing.

Figure 38

FIVE

One of the most difficult cards, and one of the reasons why some people find the Rider pack too negative. And yet it mirrors a real situation that most people will experience at some time in their lives.

All the Fives show conflict or loss. Swords carry this idea to the extreme of defeat. Sometimes the meaning of the card will focus on the large figure in the foreground – the victor. More commonly we identify with the two figures turned away. They have lost some battle, and now the whole world bears down on them – the water choppy, the sky jagged. A sense of humiliation as well as weakness goes with their defeat.

The image of an enemy can refer to a real person, to an overall situation or to an inner feeling of inadequacy. Once I did a reading for two people who had suffered at the hands of a disturbed and vengeful boss, and who now wanted to know if they should bring him to court. They decided against it when the Five of Swords indicated they would lose. Later two other people did sue the man for the same kind of misconduct. They lost the case.

REVERSED

The painful quality remains, though the emphasis may shift.
Where right side up indicates the moment of defeat, reversed
extends this to the despair felt afterwards. It is a difficult state
to overcome, though other influences, particularly those symbolized by Wands, may help.

Swords are more pessimistic than any cards in the Major
Arcana. Taken alone, no Minor suit can show the true
balance of life. They break experience into parts and therefore
distort and exaggerate. An excess of Swords cards needs more
than any other suit to be balanced with experiences and
attitudes from the other suits elements.

Figure 39

FOUR

Fours relate to stabilization; for the unhappy Swords this
translates as rest or even just retreat. The image shows not
death but withdrawal. People sometimes respond to
difficulties by isolating themselves, literally hiding in their
houses, or simply flattening their emotional reactions to hide
inside themselves. This card once appeared in a reading for a
man accustomed to dealing forcefully with everyone around
him. The card showed him that when his aggressiveness
failed, or when his confident mask grew too heavy for him, he
hid from the world rather than show his other side or try to
work with other people.

Withdrawal, however, can also lead to healing, if the purpose is not to hide but to recoup strength. The card can mean holding back from a fight until there is a better chance of winning. Similarly, by withdrawing for a time after some deep hurt a person gives him or herself a chance to recover.

Notice that the knight lies in a church, and that the window shows Christ giving a healing blessing to a supplicant. The imagery suggests the Fisher King of the Grail legend, whose physical wound mirrored the spiritual sickness of the kingdom. The picture also recalls Sleeping Beauty. Both these figures needed outsiders to awaken them. The King lay ill until Galahad brought the Grail's blessing; and the princess, symbol of a neurotic fear of life, remained asleep until the prince, refusing to be stopped by the fence of thorns (the neurotic will use the force of her or his personality to set up barriers against other people), roused her through sexual life-energy (in the Disney version he kisses her; in folk tales he has intercourse with her). Withdrawal, even for the purpose of recovery, can shut a person off from the world, creating a kind of spell only outside energy can break.

REVERSED
Reversed this card shows a return to the world. Whether this comes about quietly or dramatically depends on the situation. Sometimes the card refers to caution, as if the knight emerges carefully from his sanctuary. At other times the Four reversed can represent other people perceiving and breaking through the fence – the prince coming after Sleeping Beauty.

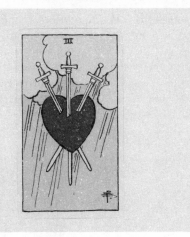

Figure 40

THREE

The Golden Dawn title for this card is 'Sorrow'. Of all the Swords, the Three most simply represents pain and heartbreak. Yet, for all its gloom, the picture brings a certain calm in the symmetry of its swords. To true sorrow we can make only one response – take the pain into our hearts, accept it and go beyond it. The Nine raised the question of how to continue after a great anguish. The Three tells us that we must not push the pain away from us, but somehow take it deep inside until it becomes transformed by courage and love.

Once, in a reading for myself, after a death in my family, the Three of Swords came up crossed by the Three of Cups. At first I thought this meant setting joy and friendship against sorrow. Two cards of the same number, however, often mean a transformation. And the crossing card often emerges from the first in some way. Looking deeper into the reading, I saw the two as connected, not opposed. Acceptance and love can turn pain into joyful memory, an embracing of life.

REVERSED
The healing process becomes blocked when we fight acceptance. If something in life appears too painful we may push it away, try not to think about it, and avoid any reminders. Such an attitude keeps the pain forever with us, and in fact

increases its hold. Waite writes: 'mental alienation ... disorder, confusion'. A reading once for a woman showed great potential for development in many areas, yet the outcome appeared very mediocre, weak. In the position of background lay the Three of Swords reversed. Earlier the woman had spoken of the ways in which she had never got over the death of her father.

(a)   Figure 41   (b)

TWO

One method of handling problems or opposition is to push everything away beyond an emotional fence. If we let nothing approach us, then nothing can hurt us. In contrast to the Eight, the blindfold here shows not confusion, but a deliberate closing of the eyes. The figure has tied it on herself so that she will not have to choose between friend and enemy, for such choice becomes the first step in once again involving herself with other people. The swords remain ready to strike anyone who tries to come close. They represent anger and fear creating a precarious balance; the one wants to strike out, the other wants to hide, and so the person remains tensed between them.

Notice, however, the effect this posture has on the woman. First of all, the crossed arms close off her heart. The imagery of blocked emotions continues in the way the grey dress seems to merge into the stone seat. At the same time the heavy swords raise the centre of gravity from the solar plexus to the chest. When a person holds in emotions the breathing becomes shallower, the body becomes rigid. Paradoxically, the attempt to stop emotion makes a person more emotional, as she or he thinks and acts not from the centre but from the constricted chest, seeing not the world, but her own image behind the blindfold.

Compare the Two of Swords to the High Priestess, number 2, in the Major Arcana. They sit in similar postures, but where the Priestess appears relaxed, tension coats the Two of Swords. A veil separates the Priestess from the waters of the unconscious hidden behind her; no veil protects the blind-folded woman from her disturbed pool of emotions. And yet that shallow pool is not the same water as that behind the Priestess.

The weight of the swords makes it easy for the woman to be tipped over into the choppy waters. Because it makes us concentrate on the emotions, a defensive attitude makes us more prone to outbursts, to anger and hysteria.

REVERSED
The balance is lost – or given up. Either the person becomes knocked over by people or problems charging her defences, or else the blindfold is given up for the purpose of either seeing truth or communicating. The latter experience can prove very emotional, even shattering if the person does not receive help from outside.

Figure 42

ACE

The final (first) Sword card returns us to the true essence of the suit – intellect. Pointing straight up for true perception, the sword pierces the crown of the material world. Wisdom leads us beyond illusions and limitations to the spiritual truth contained within life. Many of the Swords cards suffer from the illusion that life contains only sorrow and pain. The mountains symbolize 'abstract truth', objective facts of existence, independent of personal viewpoint and experience. The Major Arcana depicts this truth for us; more than any other Minor card the Ace of Swords reaches through to the fifth element. However, intellect alone, divorced from intuition, will only lead to more illusion. We need the Ace of Cups, that is, love, to find the truth; yet only intellect can take us beyond immediate experience.

Many people maintain that only our emotions express the real us, that emotional reactions alone will lead us to the truth. Often, however, emotions are exaggerated, egotistic, or self-indulgent. But neither will intellect alone bring real awareness. Both truth and awareness must come from a deeper level of spiritual values and experience. And so the hands come from clouds, leading us back to Spirit.

The symbolism of truth holds for mundane experiences as well. In confusing, emotional, or oppressive situations, the mind can pierce the fog and knots to give a clear understanding of the real facts. Truth expresses the Ace in its most valuable form. On another level the card signifies simply emotional force, both love and hate, in extreme forms. Notice the tight grip. The emotions, too, are a gift, enabling us to experience life intensely, but they always remain hard to hold and harder still to direct.

REVERSED
The grip fails, bringing illusion, confused ideas and feelings, overpowering emotions. The more violent feelings overcome the benevolent ones. Without a clear sense of reality, the mind can fall prey to mistakes created by emotion. Problems become exaggerated; everything, including attractions, appears to be more important than it actually is. In such situations, the Ace of Swords reversed tells us to take hold of ourselves and try to find a balanced sense of reality.

Chapter 4.
Pentacles

Our culture has a long history of despising the physical world. We see Adam's creation out of clay as a humiliation – 'ashes to ashes, dust to dust'. We insult people by 'treating them like dirt'. Emotions and abstract thoughts are seen as 'higher' than anything which actually exists. And yet, just as a painting is the end result of an artist's conception, so we can see the mortal world as the product of God's creative force. For us, creation means the world of our senses. However far we may travel in spiritual meditations we must begin and return *here* – or lose ourselves in the process.

A famous Qabalistic tale illustrates this need for 'grounding'. Through study and meditation four rabbis entered Paradise. Rabbi Ben Azai experienced such ecstasy that he fell dead on the spot. Rabbi Ben Zoma, overwhelmed by the flood of experience, went mad. Rabbi Ben Abuysh saw what looked like two Gods, a contradiction of the basic tenet of monotheism, and thereby became an apostate. Only Rabbi Akiba entered and left in peace. We can explain this story in terms of Tarot symbolism. Rabbi Ben Azai went too far in the direction of Fire and so burned himself out. Rabbi Ben Zoma allowed his emotions (Water) to overcome his reason. Rabbi Ben Abuysh, overbalanced with Swords energy, took both what he saw and what he read in the Scriptures too literally. Rabbi Akiba, able to balance the other elements in Earth, understood his experience in the true way.

In its earlier form of Coins, Pentacles stood primarily for materialism in the narrow sense of money and work. We still see these important qualities in the Rider pack, and indeed Pentacles carry the problem of becoming so involved with these things that we forget anything else exists – the reverse, in a way, of Rabbi Akiba. The Rider pack, however, adds the greater dimension of nature to the fourth suit. We ground ourselves not just in our work but in a love for the world around us.

As a magical sign, Pentacles symbolize the 'magic' of ordinary creation. Taken simply this means the beauty of nature, the joy of satisfying work. The symbolism, however, carries a deeper meaning, hinted at in the story of Rabbi Akiba. The mystic or magician does not simply ground the self in a negative way, using the world as the opposite of spiritual experience. Rather, the natural world, because it carries a firmer reality than the other elements, because it does not lead so easily to confusion or misconception or ill use, opens the way to more mystic experience.

The very mundaneness of day-to-day life ensures, by a kind of law of reciprocity, that such things possess a greater 'magic' than the more immediate attractions of the other elements. We cannot understand this paradox immediately. We need to ponder and experience it. Two facts about Pentacles/Earth will hint at its true value. First, in a study of religious leaders, ancient and modern, the astrologer Ronnie Dreyer has found that Earth signs predominate throughout their charts. Second, Pentacles contains more Gate cards than any other suit.

(a)   *Figure 43*   *(b)*

KING

The mundaneness of Pentacles goes very well with the social responsibility of the King, who presents to us the very image of the successful business or professional man. The casual way he sits on his throne, the fond way he looks at his pentacle – here the symbol of his capabilities and his achievements – show him satisfied with life. He is generous, even courageous, though not especially given to adventure. The role of King does not frustrate him as it does the Kings of Wands and Cups. Perhaps at an earlier stage of his life and career he might have suffered from impatience or doubt. Now his success has justified his life, allowing him to relax and enjoy it.

Enjoying life means a closeness to nature as well. Though his castle – symbol of his dominant place in society – rises in the background, he sits in his garden, with flowers on his crown, and with grapes – symbol of life's sweetness – decorating his robe. The very leaves and flowers seem to merge with his robe, just as the water flowed into the Queen of Cups' dress. Life is good to him and he means to enjoy it.

A Tarot reading once produced the Fool crossed by the King of Pentacles (the two cards greatly resemble each other in their colour schemes). The conjunction forms a fine example of what I call vertical and horizontal time, that is, the inner and outer worlds. The King symbolizes ordinary activity, accomplishments, social position, success, while the Fool stands for the inner spiritual freedom that allows a person to enjoy these things and build upon them without getting trapped in a narrow materialist view. Consider two people with the same outer worlds – both successful, respected, wealthy; yet inwardly one may be tense, or frustrated, or afraid, while the other remains joyful and at peace.

If we see the Fool as the beginning of the Major Arcana, the King of Pentacles as the final card of the Minor, then the two stand at opposite ends of the Tarot. But this polarity holds true only if we see the cards in a line. If we envision them in a circle, then the Fool and the King of Pentacles become joined together.

REVERSED
The King is meant for success. Reversing him suggests failure or simply mediocrity. The lack of fulfilment brings dissatisfaction, feelings of weakness, and doubt. Taken another way we can see the upside down King as symbolizing the idea of success corrupted, the image of a man or a woman who will use any means to achieve his or her goals.

If we describe the King of Pentacles as someone who needs a vital connection with nature (and not everyone does, despite contemporary assumptions), the King reversed stands for the state of being cut off from that rejuvenating flow. Here too the break results in dissatisfaction, weakness, even psychic danger.

(a)   Figure 44   (b)

QUEEN

Where the King sits before a castle the Queen's throne stands entirely in a field, framed by roses. Where the King simply glances at his Pentacle, the Queen holds hers in both hands, intensely aware of the magic in nature and the strength she derives from it. More than any other Minor card she represents a love for and unity with the world. The rabbit in the lower right-hand corner stands not only for sexual fertility, but also for the spiritual fruitfulness of a life that has found its own rhythm in the world around it.

Her qualities, as well as the sexual symbolism, relate her to the patron of Pentacles, the Empress. At the same time, as a Minor figure she carries a quality lacking in the archetypal trump of passion: self-awareness. She knows and believes in herself, and in the magic of her life. In readings, this quality of self-trust will often prove the most important.

If the King stands beside the Fool then the Queen belongs with the Magician. Like him she wears a red robe over a white shirt; leaves and flowers frame both of them; a yellow sky shines behind each. Where the Magician manipulates the forces hidden in the world, the Queen of Pentacles joins herself to those forces, allowing them to flow through her into her daily life.

REVERSED

In readings, the Queen reversed can mean not trusting oneself in some specific situation. More generally it refers to psychic weakness. For cutting off the Queen from her vital connection to the earth results, even more so than with the King, in nervousness and confusion. She becomes afraid, even phobic, mistrustful of others and especially of herself, doubting her abilities and her value as a person. This separation means more than being isolated from plants and animals. Rather it means a loss of daily rhythm in life, a dissatisfaction with the whole environment, and an inability to appreciate what the environment has to offer.

In a reading the Queen reversed not only points out these qualities in the subject, but suggests a dual remedy. First, a build up in confidence; besides emphasizing his or her accomplishments and good qualities a person can do this through meditation with the Queen right side up. Second, a grounding of the emotions in natural things, ordinary pleasures, satisfying work.

Figure 45

KNIGHT

The Knight's responsibility for action brings out the suit's practical qualities. At the same time, denying the Knight's natural penchant for adventure tends to distort and narrow his attitude to life. He is responsible, hardworking, uncomplaining. In his best sense he is deeply rooted to the outer world and to simplicity, a quality suggested by the way his horse stands firmly on the ground, with its rider sitting upright.

Though he also holds a pentacle he does not look at it, but instead stares over it. The symbolism suggests that he has lost sight of the source and meaning of his strength in life. In dedicating himself to purely practical matters, he has cut himself off from the deeper things in Earth.

REVERSED
Sometimes the Knight reversed can mean an awakening of those other awarenesses. More often it shows a failure – or exaggeration – of the Knight's more obvious virtues. His steadiness slows down to the point of inertia, his plodding responsibility gives way to idleness. A mild personality, taken just a little too far, becomes weak and depressed, especially if his placidity has covered a repressed desire for either adventure or greater advancement.

The Knight of Pentacles reversed can sometimes indicate a crisis. If a person has dedicated her or his life to a job or some similar outer responsibility, and that meaning is taken away – say through dismissal or retirement – then discouragement and depression can overcome him or her. Another example would be a woman who has dedicated her life to her children and now finds that they have grown up and away from her.

Though such extreme meanings of course occur rarely in actual readings, they remain implied in the Knight's basic paradox: deeply grounded in, yet unaware of, the magic beneath him, he identifies himself with his functions. He needs to discover the real source of his strength, within himself and in life.

Figure 46

PAGE

In direct contrast to the Knight the Page looks at nothing but his pentacle, holding it lightly in the air. Where the Knight is the prototypical worker the Page represents the student, lost in his studies, fascinated, feeling little concern for anything outside them. Nevertheless he partakes of the suit's practical nature by symbolizing the actual work of the student, the study and scholarship, as compared to the inspiration symbolized by the Page of Cups.

The student here acts as a symbol; the Page need not refer to someone actually in school, but simply anyone approaching any activity with those qualities of fascination, of involvement, of caring less for rewards or social position than for the work itself.

REVERSED

Again the Page appears as the converse of the Knight. In reality the two of them split the Pentacles double qualities – practicality and magic. Where the Knight, without his job, becomes discouraged and inert, the Page, without his sense of hard work, gives way to wildness and dissipation, what Waite calls 'prodigality'. Sometimes, however, the card can mean simply relaxation after a difficult task, like a student unwinding after examinations.

Figure 47

TEN

One of the most symbolic and deeply-layered Minor cards, the Ten shows us the very image of the Gate opening to hidden experience in ordinary things. Like the Ten of Cups it deals with domestic life, but where the men and women in Cups celebrate the gift, the family here does not notice the magic all around them. On the surface the card represents the established home, the good life, a secure and comfortable position in the world. The people concerned, however, appear to take the comfort for granted; they find the security boring or stifling. In contrast to the Ten of Cups (the two cards will often appear together in readings) the family here does not seem to communicate with each other. The man and woman face opposite ways, though the woman glances anxiously over her shoulder at the man. The child hangs on nervously to its mother, but looks away. And none of them notices the old man outside the arch.

Though the card expresses mundaneness, magic signs cover it. The ten pentacles form the Qabalistic Tree of Life, something which appears nowhere else in the deck. Notice also the magic wand resting against the arch; no other Minor card contains one. The arch itself bears a relief of balanced scales (just above the old man's head). Now, scales stand for Justice, and further, for subtle forces which keep the everyday world from breaking into chaos. By 'subtle forces' I do not mean only so-called 'occult' laws, such as polarity, or the law of correspondences (as above, so below). The term applies also to nature's generally more accepted workings, such as gravity, or electro-magnetism. Because we learn about these in school we should not consider such phenomena as any the less marvellous. The fact is, we all take the universe for granted simply because it works so well.

Even more than the other images, the old man evokes magic. He resembles the image, from every culture, of the god or angel who comes disguised as a beggar or traveller to visit some family, test their virtues of hospitality and generosity, and then leave them a magical gift. In the case of Abraham and Sarah the angels gave them a son, Isaac. In many such stories only the dogs recognize the visitor (just as in other tales the dogs alone run from the Devil when he comes in disguise). Because they have not buried their instincts in blasé human rationalism, the dogs can sense the wonderful when it comes to call.

Now, most of these tales emphasize the moral 'Be nice to everyone. You never know whom you might turn away'. But we can give the story a more subtle interpretation. By acting a certain way, people create *in themselves* the ability to recognize and receive the blessings in the world around them.

All these hidden signs and wonders point up the basic theme of Pentacles: the everyday world contains a magic greater than any of us can usually see. The magic is all around us, in nature, in the very fact that life exists and that this vast universe does not fly apart.

Inside the arch we see a bright ordinary day; outside darker tones prevail, even in the old man's coat of many colours, with its signs of astrology and ritual magic. The family stand under the arch posed as in a play. For all its firm reality, the everyday world, the comfortable lives we take for granted, and even the troubles and miseries that often occupy our minds, are only a play, in which we all follow the parts set out for us by our upbringing and by society (the recognition that we are a product of our conditioning is the first step to freeing ourselves from it).

The true reality remains ancient, dark, and mysterious. Though we look through the arch the perspective of the card places us outside it, with the demon visitor. By merging with this card we can find ourselves beyond the Gate, looking in at the little dramas of our own daily lives. By going further with it we can experience that wild vibrant universe existing in the very centre of the ordinary.

When the hero Odysseus arrived home from his wanderings in the wild, monster-ridden world outside civilized Greece, he came disguised as a beggar. Only his dog recognized him. Though he wore rags, they were glorious rags (much like the visitor's patchwork coat) for the goddess Athena had given them to him. Odysseus returned to the domestic world from the wild; he destroyed the evil in his house and re-established the moral order. Yet first he had to experience what lay beyond. The Ten of Pentacles takes us there as well.

REVERSED

If the sense of boredom with life increases it can lead to taking risks, especially financial or emotional ones. Sometimes, depending on the contexts or the projected results, the risks are justified; for instance, the Fool beside the Ten of Pentacles would urge the gamble. At other times the risks come less from need than from impatience with what we already have. This situation becomes more pointed when the Ten of Pentacles appears with the Ten of Cups.

The parallel with Odysseus stands out when the card becomes reversed. Most of that hero's troubles arose because of a streak of recklessness that made him do wild things at just the wrong moment. The urge to gamble stood in opposition to his basic qualities of caution, skill, and foresight. And yet the wildness maintained the balance. Without it Odysseus would not have seen the world beyond the home and family to which he finally returned.

(a)   *Figure 48*   (b)

NINE

As material cards Pentacles deal with success and what it means in a person's life. Unlike the figure in Ten the woman here is sharply aware of the good things in her life. Her hand rests on the Pentacles, her thumb hooks on a grapevine. Awareness is one of the card's basic meanings, especially self-awareness and the ability to distinguish what matters in life, what goals truly demand our best efforts. The card signifies success – but not simply the material benefits; it means as well the sense of certainty that comes with knowing one has made the right choices and followed them with the necessary actions. The pentacles growing on the bushes symbolize a life that is productive and alive.

'Success' here means not so much worldly achievement as success in 'creating' ourselves out of the material given us by the circumstances and conditions of our life. And 'certainty', in its strongest sense, means more than looking back and seeing that we have done the right thing. It also means the ability to *know* where others can only guess. The Nine of Pentacles stands as the emblem of this quality, the true mark of the evolved person (for a further discussion see the end of the section on Readings); study and meditation with this card will therefore help achieve such certainty.

We have seen that the Nines show compromises and

choices. This theme emerges in Pentacles as well. The woman stands alone in her garden. To achieve what she has, she has had to give up normal companionship. In readings, this symbolism does not mean that the card inevitably advises giving up a relationship; but it does call for self-reliance and a certain loneliness in pursuit of goals.

The image in Fig. 48(b), slightly different from the official Rider version (Fig. 48(a)), comes from an American edition of several years ago. In this Nine of Pentacles a shadow darkens the woman's face, as well as the grapes on the card's right-hand side. Clearly she is turning away from the sun. The symbolism suggests a sacrifice. To make of her life what she wants she has had to give up not only companionship, but also such things as spontaneity, wandering, and recklessness. If the sacrifice seems too great, it perhaps means that we do not value enough the rewards of self-development.

The image of the bird carries these ideas further. A soaring hunter, the falcon symbolizes the intellect, the imagination, the spirit. The hood, however, subdues it to its mistress, that is, the conscious will. Therefore, while at first glance the card means success, a more intimate knowledge of it shifts the primary meaning to that of discipline. And an entry through the Gate of this card will help bring one to the joy of true discipline, which does not cripple, but soars.

REVERSED

The qualities of the card become denied or turned around: lack of discipline and the failure that comes from it; projects taken up and then abandoned; an inability to channel energy into useful purposes. It can mean not knowing what we want, or what really matters to us. The lack of self-awareness brings irresponsibility and faithlessness, to others as well as ourselves.

Figure 49

EIGHT

The way to Spirit for Pentacles lies not so much in success, or even awareness of value in ordinary things, as in the work that allows us to appreciate those things. The Nine shows discipline; the Eight shows the training that brings both discipline and skill.

Work, whether physical, artistic, or spiritual (the Sufi Idries Shah speaks of 'work' as the most basic of Sufi doctrines), cannot succeed if the person thinks only of the end result. Many artists and writers have testified to this fact, warning hopefuls that if they just want to become famous or rich they will never succeed. We have to care about the work itself.

Therefore we see the apprentice lost in his task. And yet work also needs to be related to the outside world. However much we follow our standards and instincts or seek our own development the work we do lacks meaning if it does not serve the community. Therefore, behind his shop – though far away – stands a city, with a yellow road (yellow for mental action) leading to and from the workshop.

REVERSED

When reversed the card suggests primarily impatience and the situations resulting from it: frustration, unfulfilled ambition, envy, or jealousy. These things may result from the attitude of looking only to success, and not to the work that brings it. They may also arise from unsatisfying work, that is, a job or career which calls for no skill, no personal involvement, no pride.

Figure 50

SEVEN

From the image of work we move to its reward. Like the Nine the Seven shows the pentacles as a living development from the person's labour. Meaningful work gives more than material benefit; the person too grows. The Seven shows that moment of being able to look back with satisfaction on something accomplished. The 'something' may be as broad as a career or as simple as an immediate project. The card implies that whatever has been built up (including relationships between people) has reached a point where it can grow by itself, and the person can step back from it without it collapsing.

REVERSED
For many people, meaningful work is simply not available. In general the Seven reversed shows the pervasive dissatisfaction, the trapped feeling, that comes from unsatisfying jobs or commitments. Again, the Seven reversed can mean any specific dissatisfaction or anxiety, in particular one arising from some project that is not going well.

Figure 51

SIX

The next two cards, related by their symbolism, stand among the most complex cards of the Minor Arcana, indeed of the whole deck. At the same time they demonstrate the difference between layers of interpretation and that extra dimension I call the Gate; for while the Five allows quite a few meanings the Six shows us the Gate mechanism itself.

On the surface the Six of Pentacles illustrates the idea of sharing, generosity, charity. Notice, however, that the people form a hierarchy, one above two others. The card therefore signifies a relationship in which one person dominates others. He or she gives, but always from a basis of superiority. The scales are balanced; such relationships are often very stable, precisely because the people are well matched. Just as one wishes to dominate, the other(s) wishes to be dominated. The lower position does not really imply weakness; the dominated person often instigates the relationship, and in fact will subtly insist on maintaining it when the one who plays the dominant role might wish to change.

Sometimes the hierarchy does not indicate a person but rather a situation – emotional, economic, or other – which dominates a person or a group of people. It may give them very little, but just enough to keep them from looking for something else. This can happen in a job which gives material benefit but little satisfaction or chance for improvement; or a relationship in which the people are unhappy but comfortable; or a political situation where people recognize they are oppressed, but do not wish to endanger what little security they have.

The card bears a (distorted) relationship to all those Major cards (the Hierophant, the Lovers, the Devil, and others) in which some force holds together or reconciles the opposites of life. Here nothing becomes truly reconciled, but the situation maintains the balance and keeps it going.

So far the meanings emphasize the two beggars. But what of the giver? He shows generosity, yet the balanced scales indicate he does not give spontaneously, but rather measures out what he thinks he can afford. In other words he gives what he will not miss. Emotionally this symbolizes a person who relates really easily to others yet always holds back his or her deepest feelings.

As we said above, the relationship comes from both sides. Many people will only accept limited 'gifts' from others. A display of strong emotions, for instance, may embarrass or scare them. The same may hold true for people who resent 'charity' and put any offer of help in that category. Therefore the Six of Pentacles may indicate *giving people what they are able to receive.*

I have emphasized these words because they imply something beyond their literal meaning. Most people will unconsciously measure out their giving according to what other people expect from them; they avoid making themselves or other people uncomfortable. On the other hand, in order *consciously* to give people what they need and can use (rather than what they may think they want) one must have achieved a great degree of self-knowledge as well as awareness of human psychology in general. Few people really reach this level of giving; many people who think they perceive what someone else needs are actually projecting their own requirements and fears onto that person. As a more objective source of information the Tarot can help us understand our own or someone else's needs. Because of these meanings, the Six of Pentacles relates to the Nine in the context of that card as an emblem of certitude.

The idea of giving what people are able to receive carries a religious meaning as well. Mystics and esotericists often say that the truth hidden within a specific religion may run almost opposite to what that religion appears to say on the surface. For instance, while doctrine may teach us to control our desires through pious thoughts, the occultist may attempt to bring forth and work with her or his most hidden urges. This split exists because most people are not only incapable of but even unwilling to deal with religious/psychological teachings in their undisguised form. Even many who try may find the truth impossible to assimilate. Consider Rabbi Ben Abuysh, who lost his faith when he thought he saw two Gods.

Idries Shah tells the fable of two men who come upon a tribe which harbours a great fear of water-melons, believing them to be demons. The first traveller tries to tell them the truth and is stoned as a heretic. The second accepts their orthodoxy, gains their confidence, and slowly works to educate them. Like this tale, the Six of Pentacles indicates the manner in which religion, and also esoteric teachings, give what we are capable of receiving. Waite, in describing this card, says 'a person in the guise of a merchant' – not a merchant, but a person 'in the guise' of one. And Nietzsche, in *Thus Spake Zarathustra,* has a hermit tell Zarathustra, 'If you want to go to them, give no more than an alm, and let them beg for that.' Give more and no one will listen.

Yet who is this person in his merchant 'guise'? Is he simply a teacher, or a religious or psychological doctrine? The scales suggest something more – Justice, which stands for truth, not just as 'correct information' but as a living force holding together and balancing the universe. In the Ten of Pentacles we saw this force as the old man at the gate; here we see it as the merchant. *Life* gives us what we need, what we can use. Especially when we put ourselves in a position to receive.

People who work with meditation or the Tarot or similar disciplines (as well as people doing artistic work) often notice a curious phenomenon. Life appears to conspire to give them what they need to help them on their way. Not a great burst, but just enough to give them a little push when they can most use it. Here is an example. At the time when I was working with these meanings for the Six of Pentacles I did a Tarot reading for myself in which the Six came up crossing the Knight of Cups. I took this to mean that by keeping a meditative frame of mind I would receive benefit. Now, this occurred some months after my mother's death, and while visiting my father I found and began to wear a *mezuzah* (a kind of Jewish amulet) of my mother's. The *mezuzah* was inscribed with the name 'Shaddai'. I recognized this word as a name of God, but did not know what it meant. Two or three days after the reading I went with my father to a synagogue for the Saturday prayers (something I would not have done on my own). On the way in I saw the name Shaddai on some jewellery on display, and mentioned my curiosity about its meaning.

When I looked at the Bible reading for that day I discovered a note explaining the meaning of Shaddai. Translated as 'Almighty' it comes from a Hebrew root meaning 'to over-power'. But it relates also to an Arabic word meaning 'benevolence, giving of gifts'. Not only did the book answer my immediate question, but it gave me a greater understanding of the Six of Pentacles. The 'merchant' symbolizes the force of life, which not only gives us what we need and can receive, but can also overpower us (yet ordinarily does not if we do not wish it) with spiritual wonder. And I had gained these insights (which, because I experienced them, meant more to me than they would have as intellectual ideas) by literally putting myself in a position to receive, that is, by going with my father to the synagogue.

From the Six of Pentacles we learn that the value of studying the Tarot or other disciplines lies not simply in the specific knowledge gained but also in the frame of mind created by the *act* of doing it. The work itself changes us. We can develop these changes consciously and deliberately through the mechanism of the Gate cards. By contemplating and joining their pictures we allow ourselves to receive their gifts.

REVERSED

The possible meanings relate to the meanings right side up. A lack of generosity, selfishness when sharing is expected. Some-times this refers to a situation where the person is in a superior position. Then the giver is challenged to give more freely, not to measure out what he or she can afford, but really to share. At other times the card will point up the resentment of those people receiving charity, or its emotional counterpart, pity.

Often the Six reversed indicates that some stable, but basically unequal or unsatisfying, situation has been disrup-ted. Whether or not this disruption results in a freer or more equal situation will depend on various factors, not least of which is the desire and courage of the people involved to continue a process which they, or some outside agency, have started.

Finally, of course, it means not putting ourselves in a position to receive; either cutting ourselves off spiritually, or missing some practical opportunity, perhaps through arrogance or suspicion of other people's motives.

(a)   Figure 52   (b)

FIVE

The various meanings for this card illustrate again that problem of certitude discussed in the section on Readings. How can we know for sure which meaning will apply in a real situation? At the same time the meanings show the way in which a situation can turn in very different directions.

The Fives illustrate conflict and loss of some kind; in terms of Pentacles this means first of all material troubles, such as poverty or illness. Sometimes it implies a longstanding hardship. Observe that the people, though bent and crippled, are surviving. This card may indicate love, especially that of two people holding together in a bad situation. It may turn out that hardship has become one of the major factors keeping them together, so that relief from their material troubles may strain their unity – or they may think this will happen and therefore fear change.

Notice that they are passing a church. Now, as a place of sanctuary, the church represents rest and relief from the storm. The people, however, do not see it. Human beings can get used to anything, and when they do they will often not see opportunities for change; they will even resist an end to their problems. If we compare these people with the kneeling beggars of Six we see that Five represents pride and independence, sometimes to a foolish degree when help is genuinely offered.

As we examine the card more closely we can discover alternative, even opposed, meanings. The card shows no door to the church. As with many real churches today, which lock their doors like businesses at 5 pm, this church has perhaps shut the people out. The sanctuary has failed. We see first of all a comment on modern religion, which many feel has failed in the task of giving comfort and healing to people's troubled souls. On a simpler level, in many countries the churches have grown rich at the people's expense. Again, compare the Five with the Six. The merchant there may symbolize the modern secular church, giving what material assistance it can (or will), while the people's spiritual needs go unattended.

We can call the previous paragraph the 'sociological' interpretation of the doorless church. If we shift the emphasis to the people we can see a psychological view. Sometimes we may find ourselves in a situation where outside forces – social institutions, family, friends, etc. – cannot help us and we must struggle against the problems on our own.

We can extend this idea to a 'magic' or occult interpretation. In Part One of this book I discussed how the magician, by setting out on a course of personal development, pits him or herself against the established Church, which traditionally acts as an intermediary between human beings and God. The choice may bring practical as well as political consequences. If the magician encounters dangerous psychic forces, then traditional religion cannot (let alone will not) help him or her overcome them. Compare the Five of Pentacles with the Hierophant, number 5 in the Major Arcana. There two supplicants submit to a doctrine that guides them in all situations. Here the people have rejected such doctrines, or have simply found them irrelevant.

REVERSED

Waite gives the meaning 'chaos, disorder, ruin, confusion'. This suggests that the situation right side up has collapsed. The people are no longer surviving. While the immediate situation may seem much worse it can sometimes lead to improvement. When people accustom themselves to suffering, a collapse may release them. Whether they now can build something more positive depends partly on themselves and partly on the influence and opportunities around them.

Figure 53

FOUR

We see first of all the image of a miser, and by extension, dependence on material comforts and security for the stability symbolized by the number Four. As if in response to the troubles shown on the previous card the man has given himself a protective layer against any economic (or other) problems that might arise in the future. However, while the Five showed two people, here we see one person, excluding others through his need for personal security.

As magic signs the pentacles symbolize basic emotional/ psychic energy. The man here uses his pentacles to close himself off from the outside world. He has covered his most vital points: the crown of the head (literally a crown here), the heart and throat, and the soles of the feet. People working with chakra meditation will recognize the first two as vital points of connection to Spirit, and to other people. Covering the feet symbolizes blocking ourselves off from the world around us. The man cannot, however, seal his back. We always remain vulnerable to life, no matter how self-centred we try to make ourselves.

In certain situations, the Four, usually viewed as a 'problem' card, becomes very appropriate. When life has broken down into chaos, then the Four indicates creating a structure, either through material things, or by turning emotional and mental energy inwards. The card remains an image of selfishness but sometimes selfishness may be precisely what is needed. People who meditate through their auras will usually, at the end of each meditation, follow a ritual of 'sealing' the aura at the chakra points. This practice prevents both a leaking of their own energy and a flooding of the self by outside influences.

Finally, on a very deep level, the Four of Pentacles symbolizes the way in which the human mind gives structure and meaning to the chaos of the material universe. This idea does not contradict the concept of forces balancing nature, as described in Ten and Six. Rather it adds to that idea, by showing that the mind not only perceives, but actually helps those forces to function. The fact that human beings exist in the universe as creators rather than as passive observers forms one of the meeting points between mystical/esoteric teachings and contemporary physics.

REVERSED
Here the energy becomes released. The act can signify generosity and freedom – if right side up indicates greed or confinement within ourselves – but it can also represent the inability to hold our life together, to give it structure. Once again, in an actual situation the meaning depends on other influences.

Figure 54

THREE

We return here to the theme of work, seen both in its literal sense and as a symbol of spiritual development. The man on the left is a sculptor, a master of his art. The card sometimes appears in connection with the Eight of Pentacles, signifying that the hard work and dedication have resulted or will result in mastery.

To the right stand a monk and an architect holding the plans of the church. Together the three figures signify that the best work combines both technical skill (Air) and spiritual understanding (Water) with energy and desire (Fire). Observe how the pentacles form an upward pointing Fire triangle, showing that work can raise us to higher levels, while below them a flower sits within a downward pointing Water triangle, symbolizing the need to root such work in the reality of the world and the needs of the community. Reflecting this duality the card, like the Nine, refers to actual work yet may also stand as a symbol of the developed self. These two meanings do not cancel each other out. As observed earlier, practical work, done consciously and with commitment, may serve as the vehicle for self-development.

Part of this card's meaning lies in the fact that such symbolism of psychic development should occur in mundane Pentacles, rather than the often more exotic images of the other suits.

REVERSED

Mediocrity: the work, physical or spiritual, goes badly, often from laziness or weakness. Sometimes the meaning extends to a general situation in which little happens; things continue, either getting worse or improving, at a slow steady rate.

Figure 55

TWO

Like the Two of Swords the Two of Pentacles strikes a precarious balance, though in general a happier one. We see, in fact, the very concept of balance in the image of the juggler. At times the card means juggling life itself, keeping everything in the air at once. More simply, it carries the idea of enjoying life, having a good time – similar to the Nine of Cups, but lighter, a dance more than a feast.

Like so many Pentacles, the card implies a hidden magic in its ordinary pleasures. The juggler holds his magic emblems within a loop or ribbon shaped like an infinity sign, the same sign which appears above the head of the Magician, and the woman in Strength. Some people believe that spiritual development occurs only in serious moments. Pleasure and amusement can also teach us a great deal, as long as we pay attention.

REVERSED
Here the game becomes forced: Waite says 'simulated enjoyment'. Faced either with some problem we do not wish to face,
or else with social pressure not to make a fuss, we may pretend
to ourselves as well as to others, to take everything lightly. The
juggling act is likely to fail.

Figure 56

ACE

The gift of the Earth: nature, wealth, security, a joyful life. On
this Ace alone we see no Yods falling from heaven. The Earth,
in its completeness and solid reality, bears its own magic.

We have seen with the other cards (primarily the Ten) how
the magic will often remain hidden from us simply because we
see its products as so ordinary. Here the hand gives its gifts in
a garden, a place sheltered from the wilderness seen beyond it.
Civilization, when it works well, gives us this basic protection.
Through the work of civilization humanity shapes the raw
material of nature into a safe and comfortable environment.

Spiritual work leads us to recognize the magic in normal
things, in both nature and civilization, and then to go beyond
them to the greater knowledge symbolized by the mountains.
The exit from the garden forms an arch very similar to the
wreath of victory surrounding the World Dancer. As the
Minor Arcana comes to an end the Ace of Pentacles shows us

once more how, when we are ready, the Gate always opens to the truth.

REVERSED
Because material gifts exist in a way that the gifts of the other Aces do not, they are more open to abuse. The Ace of Pentacles reversed can signify all the ways in which wealth corrupts people – selfishness, extreme competition, mistrust, overdependence on security and comfort.

Taken another way the garden can sometimes stand for protection, either by events or other people, from the problems of life. Reversed then indicates that this protection has ended, and that the person must deal with her or his problems; or that the person wishes to hang on to this shelter after the time has come to leave it. Like the Hermit reversed, it can symbolize a refusal to grow up – specifically, to become independent of our parents.

At other times, however, the Ace reversed can mean recognizing (as with the Eight of Cups) that the time has come to leave the familiar behind and travel through the Gate to the mountains of wisdom.

READINGS

Chapter 5.
Introduction to
Tarot Divination

The use of Tarot cards for doing readings – 'divination', to give the practice its proper name – has been controversial for at least as long as the occult, 'serious' study of the cards began in the eighteenth century. Paradoxically, while many occultists will sneer at divination, most people know of no other purpose for Tarot.

Fairly early in their history, Tarot cards came into the hands of the Romany, or 'gypsies', probably when they entered Spain from North Africa (the cards apparently came to Spain from Italy or France). The Romany have given us no information on any private or secret use they might have made of the cards. Publicly, of course, they used them to make money telling fortunes – for the rich in private chambers where no one could learn their secrets, for the poor in tents and caravans at fairs and festivals.

Many people today still believe the Romany invented Tarot, despite clear evidence to the contrary. The connection between the two remains so strong that many women wishing to read professionally will dress in bright scarves and flouncing skirts and gold earrings (balloon pants and brocaded vests and *one* earring for men) and take names like 'Madam Sosostris' in order to satisfy the public.

The long association of Tarot reading with cheap theatricals probably explains, at least in part, the contempt or lack of interest many Tarot students have shown towards divination. Seeing the Tarot as both a diagram and a tool of conscious evolution, occultists and esotericists will automatically dismiss the use of the cards to usher in 'tall dark strangers' or mysterious inheritances. And yet, by seeing only the abuse and not the deeper possibilities in readings, these occultists have themselves limited the Tarot's true value.

Here is Arthur Edward Waite commenting on divination in his book *The Pictorial Key to the Tarot:* 'The allocation of a fortune-telling aspect to these cards is the story of a prolonged impertinence.' This brings us to an interesting paradox. Because they looked down on fortune-telling, Waite and others have extended the misuse of readings. The derogatory way in which they wrote about it has fixed in many people's minds the image of trivial attempts to predict the future. As to why they wrote of it at all, we can only guess that they or their publishers assumed the public demanded such an approach. After all, even today most people who pick up a book on Tarot care more about mysterious messages than they do about achieving psychic transformation. Certainly the best-selling Tarot books give the simplest formulas for the cards' meanings – and at the same time promise all knowledge.

More important than why they bothered to write about it is the simple fact that few esotericists have done much to dispel the image of divination as trivial. This disregard has even extended to the entire Minor Arcana. Because the Minor cards are associated with readings many serious books on Tarot treat them very lightly, if at all (Waite's remark applied only to the Major cards). Paul Foster Case's book *The Tarot* gives only the barest formulas in a kind of appendix at the back. Many others treat only the Major cards. Almost alone of modern esoteric studies Crowley's *The Book Of Thoth* goes deeply into the Minor cards, linking them to a complex astrological system.

As for methods of doing readings, the most important esoteric studies have given only the barest information, a few 'spreads' or designs for laying out the cards, with formula explanations for the different positions. Again, Crowley is the exception, presenting a characteristically complicated system of readings via an astrological 'clock'.

The impact of depth psychology and humanistic astrology has led many contemporary writers to seek a more serious use of divination. Unfortunately, by treating readings in such an offhand manner, the earlier writers have created a tradition of formulas which modern writers have found hard to shake off. Thus we still find the same sorts of explanations for the Minor cards, such as 'All is not yet lost; good fortune is still possible' (Douglas); and the same brief descriptions of spreads, with explanations such as 'best possible outcome' for the positions. Following Crowley and others, several contemporary books have attempted to widen the meaning of the cards by linking them not only to astrology and the Qabalah but to the I Ching, Jungian psychology, Tantra, even Central American mythology. Such linking aids understanding, particularly for those people with a previous knowledge of the other system (it would be interesting to see a book about, say, gestalt psychology which explains its subject in terms of Tarot correspondence rather than the other way round). Still, the emphasis for any careful study of Tarot must remain with the cards themselves, and with their use in meditation and in readings. This section of the book hopes to give at least a sense of just how complex and deeply instructive a tool Tarot divination can be.

COMMON SENSE

Many people say that Tarot readings 'scare' them. What they mean by this is first a discomfort that anything should expose their experiences, as well as their inner fears and their hopes; and second, that a pack of cards should do so. They may approach the Tarot first as a game, especially if a friend or relative lays the cards so that they do not have to pay for the reading. They mix the cards, grinning a little, for they feel foolish; the reader lays them out, perhaps looking up the meanings in a book, and amazingly, out comes the new job, or the unfaithful lover or, if the reader approaches it a little more subtly, perhaps the fear of illness or a painful rebellion against a parent. 'You're making that up from what you know about me,' they say, or 'You could tell all that from looking at me, couldn't you? You didn't really get that from the cards.' And then the next time someone suggests laying out the cards they laugh and say, 'No thanks, that stuff scares me.'

The fact is, the future does scare most people. They do not expect anything good to happen. They will settle for things staying the same – a balance of pain and happiness with a large measure of boredom, frustration, and low-level misery; but even such stability appears unlikely. In most people's eyes things can only get worse, and probably will.

Tarot readings teach us many things beyond the particular information we get from them. One of these is the predominance of pessimism. If a person's cards all come out positive, glowing with promised happiness, the person will probably say, 'Oh yes? I'll believe it when I see it.' But if just one card hints at trouble or illness the response changes to 'I knew it, I knew it. What am I going to do?' With such an attitude, imagine how the fear, and perhaps resentment, rises when the dread information comes to them from a pack of cards.

There is another side to this question of accepting the cards. People who go to Tarot readers often do so with a 'show-me' attitude. Since they look at divination as something 'magical' (though not really knowing what that means) they want the reader to demonstrate magical powers. The value of the reading for them lies in how accurately it matches what they know to be true about their lives, plus, of course, a bit of fresh information. To make sure the reader is 'honest', they conceal as much of their lives as possible. I remember one woman who came for advice about her work. Throughout the reading she stared blankly at me or the cards, giving me no indications at all if what I said meant anything to her. Afterwards, however, she went over every card, explaining how it related directly to her current experience.

Another time I had promised to do a Tree of Life reading (see below) for a friend as a present for her twenty-first birthday. When she told someone at work she was going to have her cards read the woman said, alarmed, 'Oh, you mustn't do that. You don't know what these people do. They go down to the city hall and look up everything about you, where you were born, where you live ...' My friend didn't tell the woman I already knew all these things.

It does not seem to occur to such people that they have wasted their time and money if they only learn things they already know, along with a smattering of new facts. They seem to forget that they have not come to test the reader but to get advice. How much more the woman could have learned about her career if she had given me the opportunity to go deeper into the relationships between the cards instead of just seeing how close I came to the facts.

Behind the fear and the scepticism lies the same problem: Tarot cards offend 'common sense', that is, the image of the world we hold in common, which is usually the image taught to us by society. We can call this image 'scientific', though only in the strict historical sense of that word as meaning the view propagated by officially recognized scientists (excluding, for instance, astrologers and yogis) since the seventeenth century. Ironically, the natural sciences themselves, particularly physics, are moving away from a strict mechanistic universe. However, culture lag ensures that most people still think of science in nineteenth-century terms.

Thus, the 'common sense' view of the world that arose in one culture – Europe – has held sway for no more than two or three hundred years, and has already started to fade. We cannot deny the achievements of this view, whatever its shortcomings. Most people who denounce science cannot offer any replacement other than nostalgia for a romanticized past that never existed. The danger which humanity now presents to nature ironically testifies to the extent to which humanity has overcome the great threats – starvation, wild beasts, disease, etc. – that nature once presented to humanity. But accepting science's achievements does not require us to banish all other contributions to human knowledge.

Modern Western science began as a consciously ideological movement, deliberately opposing the religious world-view of its time. Its early practitioners and theoreticians, such as Francis Bacon, saw themselves as revolutionaries, proposing a whole new relation to nature, one that would do more than increase knowledge. Science, they preached, would create a new world. Even today, the institution of science retains a dogmatic evangelist character. The fame and popularity of Immanuel Velikovsky derived, at least in part, from the hysterical attacks on him by scientists (in Holland, land of tolerance, scientists attempted to get the government to ban Velikovsky's books). And witness the organization recently formed by Carl Sagan, Isaac Asimov, and others for the purpose of attacking the popularity of astrology.

Interestingly, while traditional science's reputation has fallen on hard times its view of the world remains mostly unchallenged. With some justification and some confusion people blame scientists for the various threats facing life on earth. And yet 'common sense' still means the world as created by eighteenth- and nineteenth-century science. Such is the power of conditioning.

How then do we characterize this 'common' (shared, ordinary) sense? Primarily it insists that only one kind of relationship can exist between events, objects, or patterns. This is the relationship of direct physical cause. If I push something it falls over. That makes sense. Does it make sense if I think about something and it falls over? Or if I push a toy model of it and it falls over?

The common-sense person says no, if events turn out that way it is coincidence, a word meaning that two or more things have a relationship in time; they have *coincided*, but have no other relationship. Causality remains restricted to observable physical action.

But science, even in its most mechanistic period during the last two centuries, had to extend this concept to dubious limits in order to explain the observable world. The earth and the other planets move around the sun. This is a demonstrable fact. We can calculate the mathematical relationships of these moving bodies to such a degree that we can discover new bodies by an irregular movement in those already known (Neptune and Pluto were discovered this way). But the facts do not explain how this happens. No giant hands push or pull the earth around the sun. Yet the regularity of the movement prevents us calling it coincidence. Therefore, scientists invented such concepts as 'natural laws' and 'force fields'. The same person who will say that it 'makes no sense' for someone to knock over a chair by thinking about it will find it perfectly sensible that 'gravity' makes the earth go round the sun.

What then of the earlier view – that of 'correspondence', where the relationship between objects and events is that of similarity? Here it does 'make sense' that someone can knock over a chair by knocking over a toy model of it. And it makes sense that the position of the planets at the time of birth should influence personality.

Actually, both these views exist side by side today, though the correspondence view remains less respectable. Certain plants resemble human organs. Various people (particularly 'new age' or alternative healers) will claim that it makes sense that these plants should help keep those organs healthy. Other people will say it makes sense that the two things have nothing to do with each other. The 'sense' of the two groups is not common at all.

Despite this uncommonness, the two views will sometimes overlap. People who wish to justify astrology to the majority often invoke the 'law' of gravity to explain the astrological influences, despite the fact that the kind of influence that each planet is said to exert depends largely on the mythological associations assigned to that planet by ancient civilizations.

Suppose we accept the earlier common sense; does that help us accept the observable fact that Tarot readings accurately reflect a person's life? We do interpret them according to correspondences – the pattern of the shuffled cards reflects the pattern of events. Nevertheless, for many firm believers in the sense of astrology the Tarot still offends. The planets form a fixed and specific pattern at the moment of birth, one determined all the way back to creation when gravity slotted them into their predictable orbits. But shuffled cards carry no such determination. Besides, the planets are mighty beings, ponderously moving through the sky. Cards can appear so trivial. How can we accept them?

For many people, the authority of astrology derives from the vastness of the cosmos and ultimately from God. It makes 'sense' that something so small as a human being should receive its personality from the vast movements of the planets. And even if it might embarrass people to say so, we know *who* set those planets and stars in motion in the first place. But only people shuffle cards. And if they shuffle them again, why, they get a new pattern. So how could the first possess any serious meaning?

Behind this last question lies a very important assumption: that only fixed patterns are real. The fact is, the correspondence world-view can tend to mechanistic attitudes as much as the natural law view does. Both beg the question of God, or first causes. Just as neither explains how the mechanism came into being, the natural laws or the patterns of the zodiac, so neither really requires us to worry about it. God may have set it all in motion, but now it works by itself. Though a good astrologer uses intuition to interpret a horoscope, the chart itself can be constructed by anyone with a little training.

The Tarot, however, is dynamic rather than determinist. No fixed rule governs how a person will shuffle the cards. And they can always be shuffled again. (I have done as many as six readings on a question and had basically the same answer every time, though with important variations, with many of the same cards appearing in every reading. The observation that something works, however, does not explain *how* it works.)

In the 1930s Carl Jung and Wolfgang Pauli decided to study 'meaningful coincidence'. Jung became interested in the subject through astrology and experiments with the I Ching – which frightened him in much the same way the Tarot frightens most people. Pauli took up the subject from a more personal involvement; coincidences seemed to follow him like a faithful, and often clumsy, dog.

Their investigations did not really go much beyond the stage of proclaiming that such coincidences exist and some sort of principle must lie behind them. They did, however, add a new word to the world's languages: synchronicity. Events are synchronous when no observable cause connects them and yet a meaning exists between them. For instance, if we need to consult a certain rare book, and without any knowledge of this need someone comes to our house carrying a copy of this book, we call this conjunction synchronous.

People often use the word 'synchronicity' as a charm against the philosophic difficulties of events which have no apparent cause. When something seemingly impossible happens we say, 'It's synchronicity' and escape the assault on common sense. Jung and Pauli, of course, saw the term as something more than that. They were trying to suggest that an 'acausal principle' could connect events as surely as the causal ones of natural laws. In other words, if we bring bits of information together in a random way, free from the causal connections of conscious direction, then the acausal synchronicity will bring them together in a meaningful way. This is, of course, what happens in divination. The important thing to notice here is that the synchronous principle can only take over if we first remove the causal one. In other words – any method of producing random patterns – shuffling cards, throwing coins – is necessary to give the principle a chance to work.

In a way, divination really derives from a world-view older even than that of correspondences. We can call this view 'archaic' and describe it as one in which God or the gods are present at all times, taking an active part in destiny and the running of the universe. In such a world nothing happens because of any laws, but rather because God chooses to make it happen. Thus, not gravity but the Great Mother causes spring to follow winter. And she may just as well choose not to make it happen.

For people who held this view, communication with the gods was not only possible but necessary. Not only did they want to keep the gods happy, or at least not angry, but it helped if they had some idea of what the gods intended. People who could not depend on the predictability of natural laws, or the measured movements of the planets, had to ask.

They could communicate with the gods in two ways. First, it was (and is) possible to go into a trance and visit the gods in their celestial retreats, as the great shamans have always done. More easily, and less dangerously, they could let the gods speak through code, that is, divination, using dice, entrails, bird patterns, yarrow sticks, cards.

But why should these random patterns constitute God's speech? As with synchronicity the answer is because they *are* random, because they *do* offend rational common sense; they bypass the ordinary moment-by-moment way in which people experience life. Like dreams, they step outside the normal logic-bound language of conscious humanity. And by stepping outside it, they transcend it.

In this archaic view God is present in all things, all events. God speaks to us all the time. Our limited perception, however, prevents us from sensing this communication. It is just as well this limitation exists. As the three rabbis who entered Paradise with Rabbi Akiba learned, God's speech overwhelms, blinds. In fact, as we saw in Part One of this book, the veil of ego exists not only as a cumbersome limitation but as a saving mercy from the true power of the universe. The purpose of esoteric training is not simply to remove the veil, but rather to train the self to make proper use of the lightning flash of God's speech. Nevertheless, if as ordinary people we want some information from God – that is, from beyond our own limited perceptions – we need a way to see round the blinkers which cut us off from the world of Truth. We need to produce synchronicity.

Any device which produces a 'random' pattern will serve this function. It is possible that all the gimmicks people use for gambling originally served for divination, and for the same reason. Dice and mixed cards and spinning wheels all cut through the conscious mind's control of the outcome.

Identifying some of the Tarot's ancient roots (I am not suggesting the Tarot itself goes back to ancient times, only that the concepts behind its working do) does not explain it to modern minds. However, certain aspects of the archaic world-view have begun to return, suitably clothed in the modern terminology of physics and depth psychology rather than the mythological language of gods and goddesses. 'Synchronicity' is one such term.

Modern quantum theory suggests that on the most basic level existence does not follow any rules or determined laws. Particles interact at random, and what we observe as natural laws are actually aggregates of probability giving the appearance of determinism, something like the way a coin flipped enough times will come out to an equal number of heads and tails, so that someone might think a 'law' of balance required even distribution. (Indeed, many people believe the 'law of averages' can order the outcome of some particular event – 'You've failed every other time, the law of averages says you've got to make it this time' – when the whole point of probability is just the opposite, that it cannot predict specific events.)

At the same time that physics is eating away at the universe of fixed laws, so modern psychology (or at least some branches of it) has begun to look at non-rational theories of knowledge. Where archaic people spoke of the 'other worlds' or the 'land of the gods', today we speak of the 'unconscious'. The terms change but the underlying experience remains: a realm of being in which time does not exist and knowledge is not limited to the images received from our senses. And the methods used to 'contact the unconscious' have not changed from those employed to listen to the gods thousands of years ago – dreams, trances (of which Freudian free association is a kind of lesser version), tossed coins.

We come to the notion that the Tarot works precisely because it makes no sense. The information exists. Our unconscious selves already know it. What we need is a device to act as a bridge to conscious perception.

As pointed out earlier, reaching this level of connection, this synchronicity of uncommon sense, does not depend on what system we use. The Tarot, the I Ching, dice, tea leaves, all really serve the same function. They produce random information. Perhaps in the future more 'modern' ways of producing random patterns will emerge. Most 'pure' might be a system of divination based on the movements and energy jumps of sub-atomic particles. For it is at this most basic level that we can see the most important implication of synchronicity, that existence does *not* follow rigid determinist laws in which all events arise from fixed causes. And yet at the same time, events have meaning. Or rather, meaning emerges from events. From all the random darting and spinning of particles emerges solid matter. From the separate actions and experiences of a person's life emerges a personality. From the mixing of Tarot cards emerges awareness.

If any device will provide meaning, why Tarot? The answer is, any system will tell us something, but the quality of that something depends on the values contained in the system. The Tarot contains a philosophy, an outline of how human consciousness evolves, and a vast compendium of human experience. Shuffling the cards brings all these values into play with each other.

We might argue that assigning a philosophy to the cards destroys their objectivity in terms of predicting events. Human values and interpretations have intruded in an otherwise.pure system. Such an idea, I think, would come from a misunderstanding of 'objectivity'. The Tarot is objective because it bypasses conscious decision, but it is not impartial. On the contrary, it attempts to push us in certain directions: optimism, spirituality, a belief in the necessity and value of change.

The meanings for the cards given in this book leave a good deal of room for interpretation by the reader. In fact, they require it. This is because the practised reader brings far more to her or his work than a detailed knowledge of the cards and their traditional meanings. Just as important is sensitivity – both to the pictures and to the person sitting there nervously and excitedly staring at the cards. A good reader does not simply repeat traditional fixed meanings. Rather, he or she will find new meanings and interpretations, will extend the patterns.

While some people desire objective readings and dislike interpretation, others argue that a reader should not use any definite meanings at all, but always work from 'feeling' the pictures at the moment. Yet to do so will limit the reader to the narrow range of his or her own perceptions. And those perceptions will always come at least partly from his or her own experiences and cultural conditioning. Very few people have reached a level of awareness where they can escape the bias of their own history. For most of us, our emotions cloud our intuition. The subconscious gets in the way of the unconscious. (See the footnote on page 157, for the difference between 'unconscious' and 'subconscious'.)

A reader who trusts feelings can be led away from the truth as well as towards it. But there is another reason why we should work with the traditional meanings belonging to the images. If we do not use the wisdom others have put into the cards, then we deprive ourselves of their knowledge and experience. Therefore, part of a reader's training lies in simply studying the cards, while another part lies in gaining a personal sense of them through practice, meditation, and creative work.

Tarot readings teach us many things. One of the most valuable is this necessary balance of objective and subjective, action and intuition. Recently experimental science has 'discovered' that the two halves of the brain do not perform the same functions; the left hemisphere (governing the right side of the body) deals with rational and linear activities, while the right hemisphere (governing the left side of the body) deals with intuitive, creative, and holistic activities. (Left-handed people would appear to function the other way round, the right side governing intuition, the left rationality.) This 'discovery' is reminiscent of the argument about whether Columbus, Leif Ericson, or St Brendan discovered America. Just as the Indians had lived there for thousands of years, so esotericists had known about the split brain for centuries.

When a person has mixed the Tarot cards the reader, if right-handed, picks them up in the left hand, then lays them down with the right. We do this to give just a little more emphasis on that necessary combination of intuition and conscious knowledge. The left hand helps channel sensitivity but we turn the cards with the right because we want the rational brain to explain the pattern intuitively.

In Part One of this book I wrote that readings partake of both the Magician and the High Priestess principles, consciousness and intuition. We can go further and say that doing Tarot readings helps achieve a balance and unity of these principles in their practical states, that of will and openness. Each time we do a reading we assert our will to impose a meaning on the patterns thrown out by chaos. The act suggests not only the Magician (number 1) but the Wheel of

Fortune (number 10). The latter card carries a vision of the world in time (remember the Wirth version of the Wheel as resting in a boat – consciousness – floating on the sea of existence). However, meaning imposed by consciousness carries true value only if we open ourselves to the pictures and the impact they make on us. Therefore, Tarot readings suggest the High Priestess (number 2), but also the Hanged Man (number 12), the image of such a close connection to life that we no longer see ourselves as separate or opposed to it. And the card that connects trumps 10 and 12 can also stand for the emblem of Tarot readings themselves: Justice, her scales forever balanced not by a careful weighing of opposites – so much intuition for so much objective knowledge – but by a living commitment to the truth.

Chapter 6.
Types of Readings

BEGINNING STEPS

The true psychic readers, who are rarer than many people think, can simply take a few cards from anywhere in the deck, lay them out in no particular pattern, and use them as the trigger for going into a trance or simply for releasing the information from unconscious sources.

For most people, however, a spread helps them find the meaning in a divination. As the cards are taken off the top of the pile the reader places them in specific positions, each of which carries its own meanings, such as 'past influence', or 'hopes and fears'. The meaning of that card then becomes a combination of the picture and the position. From the symbolic meanings of all the cards a whole pattern will (we hope) emerge.

Whatever spread the reader uses, first comes the mixing of the cards and before that the choice of one card to represent the subject, or 'querent' as many writers call the person mixing them. We choose the querent card and set it aside for two reasons. First, so that the person shuffling can focus on the picture to keep the attention from wandering. Second, so the deck will then reduce to seventy-seven which is seven, the number of will, times eleven, the number of balance.

Some writers suggest using the Fool to represent the querent in all readings. Often, readers will choose some other Major card, depending on their favourites. I usually discourage this practice on the ground that the Major cards symbolize archetypal forces, whereas the subject is a whole person, existing in a specific time and place. Besides, removing a trump from the deck removes the chance of having that card come up somewhere in the reading.

Most readers prefer to use one of the court cards to signify the querent. Traditionally, the Pages have stood for children (some people see the cutoff between childhood and adulthood as the loss of virginity), the Knights for young men, the Queens for women, and the Kings for older, more mature men.

People who have read Waite's *Pictorial Key* will remember his confusing assignation of Knights to men above forty, and Kings to younger men. This system comes from the Golden Dawn Qabalistic Tarot. In that deck the Knights represent Fire, and Fire, as we might expect from an order of magicians, stands at the head of the suits. Therefore, the Golden Dawn Knights represent mature men. But the Golden Dawn deck (and Crowley's Thoth Tarot) does not contain Kings, or for that matter, Pages, at all; it uses Knight, Queen, Prince, and Princess. It makes sense for a Prince to represent a male younger than a Knight. It does not make sense for a King to do so, and most readers do not follow Waite's instructions on this point, even when using his deck.

The traditional system contains a symbol for a young man, but none for a young woman. Since women jump from childhood to full maturity no more abruptly than men do, I have found it valuable to make the Knights serve either gender, as the Pages do. In fact, since the Kings and Queens symbolize different values and approaches to life, they too may signify either a male or female questioner. A former student of mine, a psychotherapist who uses Tarot as an approach to her clients' problems, follows this practice. Unless I see a clear indication otherwise I generally choose a Queen for a woman, a King for a man. I remember one man, however, who struck me forcibly as the Queen of Swords, with her great sense of sorrow. When I showed him the card and described it he agreed completely.

Once the reader and client have decided on the figure, they must choose the suit. Usually the reader does this, following one of two methods. The first is colouring. Wands, or whatever suit stands for Fire, represent people with blonde or red hair, Cups light-brown hair and light-brown or hazel eyes, Swords dark-brown hair and eyes, Pentacles black hair and eyes. It does not take much thought to see the drawbacks of this system. Besides its general arbitrariness it makes most

Chinese people Pentacles, most Swedes Wands, and so on.

A more objective system uses astrological signs. As described earlier, the four elements signify signs of the zodiac, as well as the suits of Tarot. Most people know their own sun signs and if not the reader can readily determine it from the birthday. Of course, most astrologers say that the sun sign constitutes only one twelfth of the person's chart and another element may dominate.

In my work I find it worthwhile to increase the subject's involvement by letting him or her choose the suit. After I have decided the level (Queen, King, Knight or Page) I remove the four appropriate cards from the deck and place them before the person. If the person knows some Tarot symbolism I ask her or him to disregard formal attributes and choose simply by reaction to the pictures.

Usually we do not interpret this 'Significator' card. It stands for the whole person rather than whatever aspects belong to that card. In some situations, however, the choice becomes important. Suppose a married woman chooses the Queen of Cups to represent herself; if the King of Cups comes up in the reading it may represent her husband, or more precisely, since the reading looks at the situation from the querent's point of view, her husband's influence on her. If the husband tends towards immaturity and/or dependence on the woman, then the Knight may appear instead of the King.

Other cards of the same suit may also stand for the subject rather than someone else. If the subject chooses the King of Wands to represent himself, then the appearance of the Queen may indicate the emergence of a more 'female' side of appreciation and receptivity. If the querent is a Knight, then the appearance of the King or Queen may represent immaturity, or regression, or a more youthful attitude.

We can call these changes 'vertical' – moving up and down in the same suit. 'Horizontal' changes are the appearance of one or more cards at the same level but from different suits. If the person chooses the Queen of Swords, then the Queen of Cups appearing in the reading may indicate a change in the person. These 'transmutations' as I call them often carry great meaning.

The question of how to interpret court cards – as someone else or as an aspect of the subject – remains for most people one of the most difficult elements of Tarot reading. Usually it takes experience and a strong feeling for the cards to help indicate the correct interpretation. Even very practised readers will often find the alternatives confusing.

After the choice of Significator comes the mixing. If the person is not asking a particular question I instruct him or her to empty the mind and concentrate on the hands, or simply on the Significator. If the reading does concern a specific question I ask the person to focus on that and even say the question out loud to fix it more firmly in the mind.

The method of shuffling does not matter, except that it must be thorough and some of the cards must become turned around to allow reversed meanings to emerge. One method I sometimes recommend is to lay the cards on the table or floor (many readers always do their readings on the silk scarf they use to wrap the deck), then with both hands scatter them all around, like a child playing in the mud. Then I tell the person to bring the cards back together. Besides its thoroughness this method carries a nice symbolism. Any Tarot reading represents a personal pattern emerging from the chaos of possible combinations. Even if we only read ten cards the whole deck bears the imprint of the person who last mixed them. By scattering the deck we return it to chaos; when we bring it back together, it carries the new pattern.

With the cards mixed the subject must separate them into three piles in the following way. Using the left hand he or she must remove a pile from the top and place it to the left, then from that pile again remove a pile from the top and lay it down on the left.

Now the reader takes over, and here again people disagree about how to put the deck back together. Some simply pick up the pile on the right with the left hand, place it over the middle pile and then put these two piles over the pile on the left. Others hold their left hand a few inches over each pile until a warmth seems to rise from one of them. They then place this pile over the other two.

Either way, when the deck has re-formed, the reader, using the right hand, begins to turn over the cards in whatever pattern he or she has decided to follow. Hundreds of patterns exist. Of the three presented here, one I made up, while the other two are variations on traditional themes. Almost any book on Tarot will give further patterns.

THE CELTIC CROSS

Over the years this pattern has proved the most popular. The Cross derives its name from its shape, a cross of equal arms (one card on each side of the centre), with four cards lined up as a 'Staff' beside it (see Fig. 59, p.147).

As we might expect, commentators disagree on the meaning of particular positions and how to describe them. Some, such as Waite and Eden Gray, provide a sort of ritual for the reader to pronounce while laying out the cards: 'This covers him' or 'This lies beneath him'. Others prefer more conventional phraseology. It does not matter which system we use as long as we remain constant. The meanings described below are the ones I use. They follow the traditional system, with certain changes.

THE SMALL CROSS

In every way of laying out the Celtic Cross the first two cards form a small cross of their own with the first one, the 'cover' card, lying directly on top of the Significator and the second lying horizontally across it.

Now, the cover card usually stands for some basic influence on the subject, a general situation or starting point for the reading. The second card, which we always read right side up, despite how it comes off the deck, represents in traditional systems an 'opposing influence', something counter to the first. In practice, this 'opposition' may actually form a second influence supporting the first.

For example, suppose the cover card was the Fool, indicating a sense of following instincts despite what may seem the more sensible practice. If Temperance crossed it, we could call it an opposition, since Temperance usually refers to caution. But if the Knight of Wands crossed the Fool, the two cards would tend to support each other, and in fact the other cards might suggest a need for a more temperate influence to balance all that eagerness.

In my work I have developed a slightly different way of looking at the first two cards, referring to them not as cover and 'opposition' but as 'Centre' and 'crossing'. For their meanings I term them the 'inner' and 'outer' aspects, or sometimes 'vertical' and 'horizontal' time, or simply 'being' and 'doing'. The Centre card shows some basic quality of the person or the person's situation. The crossing card then shows how that quality affects the person, or how it translates into action. Put another way, the first shows what the person is, the second how he or she acts.

Consider the example in Fig. 57. The Fool would indicate a person with an inner tendency to take chances, to follow instinct. Temperance crossing it would mean that when it comes to action the person tends towards a more careful approach, blending instinctive energy with more practical considerations.

Figure 57

Another example will help illustrate this most valuable part of a Celtic Cross reading. The Ace of Cups in the Centre would indicate a time of happiness in a person's life, or more precisely a chance of happiness, since the Aces represent opportunities. If the Ten of Cups crossed the Ace the two would imply that the person recognizes the opportunities and will use them. But if the Four of Cups should cross the Ace a different meaning will emerge, showing an apathetic attitude that prevents the person appreciating what life offers him or her. The apathy, however, would not cancel out the opportunity.

I have stressed the small cross because of its importance. In some readings the first two cards can tell the whole story, with the others filling in details. As described in Part One the terms 'vertical and horizontal time' derive from symbolic interpreta-

tions of the crucifixion, where Eternity, embodied in Christ as
the Son of God, intersected the 'horizontal' movement of
history, that is, the death of one human being. For Christian
mystics the fact of the crucifixion allows them – through
meditation on the cross and other methods of identification
with Christ – to bring a sense of 'vertical' time into the
horizontal facts of their own physical existences. In many
other cultures the image of a cross symbolizes the four
horizontal directions along the surface of the earth, while the
centre, the meeting place of the four, suggests the essentially
vertical direction of the centre. The cross, therefore, also symbolizes the Tarot itself, the four arms being the four suits and
the centre the Major Arcana.

In terms of readings, the cross symbolism can show the way
in which a person's substance, or inner being, can mix with
the way that person acts in the world. It is worth repeating
here the original example which suggested the symbolism of
crossed time. The reading was done for a man unsure of the
direction of his life. A long love affair was ending, his chosen
career as a professional singer had not materialized. The
reading began with the High Priestess crossed by the Hierophant. Now these cards, sometimes called the Papess and the
Pope, at first glance represent contradictory values. The High
Priestess stands for instinct, mystery, stillness, while the
Hierophant, as the preacher of a doctrine by which people
may guide their lives, stands for orthodoxy, planned
behaviour, clarity. Therefore, it appeared that the two symbolized conflicting approaches to life. The more I looked at
them, however, with their religious imagery, the more I
thought of conjunctions, rather than opposites. The two
seemed to prescribe almost a way of dealing with life. The
High Priestess indicated that within himself this man carried
qualities of instinct and understanding that might never fully
emerge but could give his life substance. The Hierophant, on
the other hand, showed that in his daily life he needed a more
rational plan of action; he needed to organize and make
definite decisions to achieve what he wanted. But these plans
and practical steps would work best if backed by his own
instincts and inner awareness rather than by socially-
acceptable ideas of proper goals and behaviour. Just as I was
trying to explain how these qualities could complement each
other the man broke in to say how he saw them as constantly

in opposition, how he swung back and forth, giving in first to his desires or simply to passivity, and then moving the other way to very directed orthodox action, such as getting a 'responsible' middle-class job rather than pursue his singing. Part of my job in the reading became to show him how these qualities could work together.

'BASIS'

After the small cross the reader places the next card directly below the Centre. This position represents the 'Basis' of the reading – a situation or event, usually, though not always, in the past, which has helped create the current situation. Because of the way our past shapes us this card can sometimes explain and tie together all the others. In one remarkable

Figure 58

reading about a woman's difficulties relating to her husband, the Emperor in the Basis position indicated that her relationship to her father still dominated her unconscious sexuality and was preventing her from working out her current problems.

Usually the Basis does not show such a broad theme, but often it does indicate a previous situation, especially if a connection exists with the number or suit of one of the first two cards. Consider these three cards: the Magician crossed by the Five of Cups, with the Five of Swords beneath them (see Fig. 58). The Magician, as the person's being, shows a strong, highly-creative and dynamic personality. The Five of Cups, however, indicates that the person is currently preoccupied with some loss so that the powerful personality has become subdued. In terms of the pictures, the Magician has covered his dazzling white and red robe in a black cloak. The Five of Swords, however, shows that the loss began as a painful and humiliating defeat. It is this defeat which has dimmed the Magician's fire. But the move from Swords to Cups shows that already a process of renewal has begun. The person can begin to see the situation as one of regret rather than shame. What makes this movement possible is the Magician qualities, currently concealed yet still active in the person's life.

'RECENT PAST'
The next card lies to the left of the small cross and bears the title 'Recent Past'. The term is really a misnomer, for the difference between this position and the Basis lies not so much in the timescale as in their impact on the person. The Recent Past refers to events or situations that affect the subject, yet have passed or are passing out of importance. Usually it does refer to recent events; sometimes, however, it can show some thing reaching far back or of great importance. In the example above, of the woman whose father affected her so strongly, if the Emperor had appeared in the Recent Past instead of the Basis, it would have indicated that the block was receding from her life, and would not affect her so much in the future.

'POSSIBLE OUTCOME'
The next card goes directly above the small cross. Some people term this position the 'Best Possible Outcome'. However, a little practice will demonstrate the narrowness of

this optimistic title. If, say, the Nine of Swords shows up here it can hardly be called the 'best' result. Therefore, like many others, I refer to this position as simply 'Possible Outcome'. Now, since we call the final card 'Outcome' people may find the two terms confusing. By 'possible' we mean first of all a more general trend that may result from the influences shown in the reading. At the moment, it remains vague and may never actually come about. It simply means the person is heading in this direction.

Sometimes the relationship between the Possible Outcome and the Outcome includes cause and effect. The Possible may result from the Outcome. As a simple example, suppose the Outcome shows the Eight of Pentacles and the Possible Outcome shows the Three. The Eight indicates that the person will go through a period of hard work and learning. The Three indicates that this effort is likely to produce the desired result of great skill and success.

Sometimes the Possible Outcome indicates a more tentative result than the Outcome. Here is an example from a reading done several years ago for a woman who had applied for a job and wanted to know her chances of getting it. The Outcome card indicated delays and suspense but the Possible Outcome showed success. When the woman went to find out, the hiring agent told her that they had hired someone else but had put her on an alternate list. Several days later he called to tell her that the someone else had changed her mind and he wanted to hire the woman. The possible had become real.

There is another way of comparing the Possible Outcome and the Outcome, especially if the two contradict each other (rather than complement, as in the examples above), or if they show a direct relationship, such as the same suit or number. In these situations I read the Possible Outcome as something that might have happened but will not. The task then is to look at the other cards for the reason why the outcome should happen instead.

Suppose the Star lies in the person's Possible Outcome, indicating that the person might emerge feeling very free, full of hope, open to life. Suppose then that the Devil comes up as the actual Outcome, indicating bondage to an oppressive situation. What has gone wrong? If, say, the Nine of Swords reversed lies in the position of Basis, this would give us a clue, for it would say that the person holds inside her or him a sense of shame and humiliation coming from past weaknesses and fears, and that the 'imprisonment' symbolized in the Nine prevents the person from realizing the potential of the Star.

These examples will help us to see that the true meaning of a Tarot reading does not come from specific cards but rather from the configurations they form together.

'NEAR FUTURE'

The final arm of the Cross comes to the right of the central pattern. Lying opposite the Recent Past it bears the title 'Near Future'. It shows some situation that the person will soon have to face. It does not carry the same totality as the Outcome; rather it forms yet another influence, in this case the influence of events. If a situation begins in a certain way but ends very differently, then the reason might lie in the Near Future bringing in some new situation or person to change the direction. On the other hand, if the Outcome is very different in character from the Near Future this might indicate that the coming situation will have no lasting effect. For example, if the Five of Wands lies in the Near Future, and the Three of Cups in the Outcome, it can indicate that the person will go through a period of conflict with friends, but that this conflict will not last long, giving way to closer ties, and cooperation. Often such information can greatly help a person come through a difficult time by reassuring him or her that it will not last. And if the opposite should appear (that is, a happy situation will give way to a bad one) the reader can simply hope that the person can use this information well. Bad news is always less pleasant to give than good.

After laying out the Cross the reader turns up the final four cards, one above the other, to the right of the Cross. The final pattern looks like this:

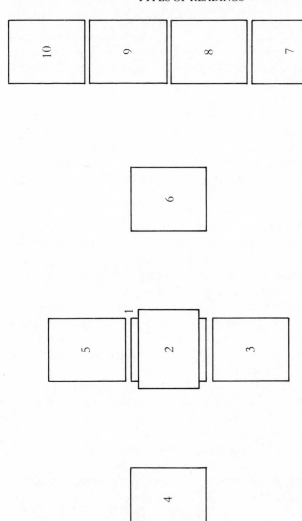

Figure 59
The Celtic Cross Pattern

1. Centre
2. Crossing
3. Basis
4. Recent Past
5. Possible Outcome
6. Near Future
7. Self
8. Environment
9. Hopes and Fears
10. Outcome

'SELF'

The card on the bottom of the Staff is called 'Self', and refers not to the whole person, but to some way in which the person her or himself is contributing to the situation. What attitudes does the subject show? What is she or he doing that will affect the situation described in the other cards? Suppose, in a reading that began with the Two of Cups, the Self position shows the Two of Swords. This would indicate that the subject finds it difficult to open up to the new relationship indicated by the first card. The subject's tense, even hostile behaviour greatly affects the overall situation. The Outcome would indicate the result of the conflict.

'ENVIRONMENT'

Just as the subject affects the reading so also do the people and general situations around him or her. We call the eighth card the 'Environment' or the influence of 'Others'. If a court card appears in this position it will usually mean a person influencing the subject. Otherwise the card can show either the effect of one important person or of a more general situation. Often it will indicate whether the environment is helping or hindering the direction in which the subject is heading. For instance, in a reading done about work, the Five of Wands reversed in the Environment would suggest that an atmosphere of hostility, trickery, and backstabbing competition is making work unpleasant.

Sometimes the Environment indicates the querent rather than other people. It shows how the subject reacts to her or his surroundings. In a reading done some time ago the Four of Swords in the Environment showed the person's habit of retreating from conflicts with the people around him.

'HOPES AND FEARS'

Above the Environment comes a position similar to Self but one with a sharper focus. We call this position 'Hopes and Fears' for it shows how the person's attitudes to the future affect the working out of events. Often this card will almost dominate the reading, especially if the Outcome is very different from the Possible Outcome, indicating that what seems likely will not happen after all. The influence shown by this card can work either for or against the person. Suppose the reading concerns a love affair, and most of the cards tend to success, with the Two of Cups as the Possible Outcome. Yet the Outcome shows the Lovers reversed, a clear sign that the relationship goes badly. If the Hopes and Fears card was the Three of Swords it would show that the person's fear of heart-break has prevented the necessary emotional commitment. At other times, a very positive card in this position, such as the Star or the Six of Wands (both cards that mean hope), would indicate that the person's attitude can create success.

Sometimes this position and that of Basis or Self will work very closely together, with the Basis explaining the origins of the subject's attitudes to the future. For instance, if the Two of Cups reversed came up as the Hopes and Fears, and Eight of Wands reversed was the Basis, it would indicate that a background of jealousy was leading to a very negative attitude towards the continuance of the love affair.

Notice in this last example that the Two of Cups reversed might be a fear, but it might also be a hope. We call the position Hopes *and* Fears rather than the more usual Hopes *or* Fears. The terminology reflects the fact that the two often go together (something originally pointed out to me by my therapist student). In work, often people hope for and fear success at the same time, while in relationships many people will fear the love they seek, or will half consciously hope for rejection. The duality of Hopes and Fears shows up most strongly in cards dealing with change, or the emergence from confined situations to open ones.

Death, the Eight of Cups, the Two of Wands reversed, and the Four of Wands all deal with these themes of freedom and change. Some others are the Devil reversed, the Eight of Swords reversed, and the Star. Very often if the subject and the reader together examine the subject's attitude to one of these images in the Hopes and Fears position, an ambivalence will emerge. Confinement is more secure than freedom. Because the unpleasant component – the fear of love (or success), or the hope of rejection (or failure) – often remains hidden from the conscious desires, the discovery of this ambivalence can help the subject work on creating what he or she really wants.

Seeing this duality at work in one reading after another teaches the reader some basic facts about conditioning. The subconscious (the repressed material we might call the lower layer of the ego – again, see footnote on page 157) is basically conservative, even reactionary. It not only resists any change, whether desirable or distasteful, it also prefers to deal with all situations in the same way it dealt with similar situations in the past. For many people each new friend or lover becomes the stage for repeating the story of Mummy and Daddy. We face each new problem or task the way we we learned to deal with problems as children. No matter if we dealt with them successfully; that counts for less than the safety of having a fixed pattern to follow. The subconscious looks first to security and then to other considerations. And security comes through repetition.

Now, this hidden mechanism of repeating past patterns has built-in survival value. When new problems arise we can handle them because the subconscious automatically compares them to previous problems and then clicks into the ready-made response. Unless a person wishes to embark on a deliberate programme of self-creation (such as the Major Arcana outlines) this system will work fairly well and probably should not be tampered with. However, if a person finds one love affair after another collapsing into jealousy and bitterness, or one job after another failing, then she or he might do well to examine the way the subconscious insists on arranging new situations to repeat the past. One way of at least beginning such an examination can be Tarot readings, with their emphasis on past experience, and what we really hope for and fear.

'OUTCOME'
Finally, the Outcome. This card brings together all the others. More, it balances them out and shows which influences are strongest, and how they work together to produce the result. Sometimes the Outcome will be an event. Then the important question becomes how it came about, not just what it is. If the subject finds it an unpleasant event, then she or he can look at the other cards to see what influences are pushing in that direction, with the hope of changing the situation. If the Outcome appears desirable then a similar study can help increase those influences, already strong, which are tending towards that result.

The Celtic Cross, like any spread, consists of a fixed number of cards. If the reader and subject find the mixture ambivalent, they can either turn over some more cards without a fixed pattern, or else do a further reading. In turning over extra cards I usually stick to no more than five (sometimes asking the subject to choose a number), though at times the initial reading has served as the basis for turning over most of the deck. Usually, beginning readers find it more difficult to interpret cards at random ?nd therefore avoid using them.

Sometimes we may do further readings to get information about a specific card in the first reading. We might have a question about a person referred to in the Near Future position. In this situation some readers will use the card in question as the Significator for the new reading. Just as the original Significator helped the person to concentrate on him or herself, so the new card helps the person focus on the particular question.

A SAMPLE READING

Before leaving the Celtic Cross I would like to present a sample reading done by me some months before writing this book. (I should state that the subject gave her consent for it to be included.)

The reading was done for a woman who had just passed her bar exam, who had recently begun a new love affair, and in general appeared happy and excited about her life. Yet when I turned over the cards I received an immediate sense of sadness. Trusting the cards rather than my conscious impressions I asked the woman if she had been feeling sad recently. To my surprise she immediately said yes.

The cards came out as follows. For the Significator the woman chose the Queen of Pentacles. The first two cards were the Three of Wands crossed by the Knight of Cups. The Basis was Death, the Recent Past the Nine of Swords, the Possible Outcome the Five of Swords reversed, and Near Future the World reversed. The Self was the Six of Cups reversed, the Environment the Three of Cups, the Hopes and Fears the Tower, the Hermit the Outcome. (See fig. 60).

I began by giving the woman a general interpretation. She was going through a time of transition when many old patterns were dying out. The effect of this was frightening as well as exhilarating. The sadness came from realizing what she had lost, and also from the fact that she had grown up and cut her ties to her childhood. The situation would not resolve

Figure 60
A sample Celtic Cross Reading

itself very quickly – there was even a chance it would develop badly, especially if she let the Near Future, showing stagnation, frighten her into a very negative attitude. The people around her, however, gave her a lot of support, even if ultimately she needed to work it out herself.

All this, of course, was very general. We then went over the cards one by one. The cover card, the Three of Wands, indicated first of all her immediate achievements, not just graduating from law school, but even going in the first place. For as we discussed what she had done she told me how before she had gone to law school she had never taken her life or her abilities very seriously. Now she had reached a point where she not only knew her own strength and intelligence, but the accomplishment of passing the bar exam on the first attempt had given her a solid base from which to look for future work. Even before we discussed these facts the meaning of them came through the image of the man standing on the cliff while sending his boats out to explore new lands.

But the Three of Wands carries another meaning, one very suited to this reading. It implies a contemplative attitude as a person looks over her memories. Actually, this looking over her life came out of the sense of accomplishment. The things she had done made her aware of how her old life had ended. At the same time the boats going out to unknown waters symbolized her situation of not really knowing what she would do next, or even what shape her life would take in the future.

The image of accomplishment and exploration bore reference to other things in the woman's life besides her career. She had recently begun psychotherapy; she had also joined a support group called 'the healing circle'. Both of these activities increased the sense of newness and the unknown, for while they gave her confidence and belief in herself they also made it much more difficult to hold on to past patterns.

Now, the Knight of Cups lay across the Three of Wands and here the second card appears very much as an outcome of the first. For the Knight of Cups signifies an involvement with oneself, with looking inward. The two cards together said that in the centre of her life the woman at that moment was contemplating the past, thinking about what her life had been, and looking to the future. But the Knight of Cups is the least connected to action of any of the Knights. When it came to practical steps she found herself very hesitant.

Below the small cross came Death, the first Major card. Death emphasized the experience of seeing the past die away. All her life the woman had maintained certain patterns: certain ways of dealing with the world, with other people, with herself. Now, because of her achievements these old ways no longer applied. Almost without warning she found herself cut off from the safe patterns without much idea of how to face the future. More about these patterns became clear as we considered cards of Self and Outcome, but here it was simply important to see that the old, whatever shape it had taken, had died.

Notice the resemblance of the Knight of Cups to Death. Since the trump lies in the Basis – the past – and the Minor card in the present, we can call the Knight a practical development from the archetype of Death. That is, underneath she is experiencing the loss of her old life, but on the surface she finds a lack of confidence, emotional as well as practical, about what to do next.

The Recent Past came directly from the Basis. It shows how the two positions can exist almost in the same time frame. In other words, the Basis did not come first and then give way to the Recent Past, but, like the small cross, the Recent Past came out of the general pattern shown by the Basis. Now, the Nine of Swords indicates sorrow, grief. It can at times symbolize mourning. In this case we can think of 'mourning' as a metaphor. The person she grieves for is herself, for we have seen in the Basis that something has 'died'. That something was not harmful, it had simply lost meaning. However, the fact that her life had gone beyond it did not stop her from missing the safe and comfortable ways of dealing with the world. Nor does the card really suggest that she misses her old self because she fears life. The sadness here is more genuine and, in fact, coexisted with the equally real joy and excitement I had seen before the reading.

The first four cards have stressed her inner life; the next two showed the Tarot's ability to indicate trends and events, and in particular to give a warning. First the Possible Outcome. The Five of Swords reversed indicates defeat, producing shame and humiliation. Its presence here showed that despite all that the woman had accomplished her efforts might still come to nothing. Now, sometimes the Outcome card will clearly contradict the Possible Outcome, showing that for some reason the possibility will not become reality. Here the relationship is more subtle. The Hermit is a good indicator that she will not lose what she has gained, but it does not guarantee anything. It shows her headed in a good direction, but not yet arriving, at least not in the practical sense. Therefore, the Five of Swords remained a possibility, and the Tarot was warning her to do what she could – use the support of her friends, not give in to her fears, especially during periods of stagnation – to avoid this result.

The World reversed stands for non-movement, a lack of success, the inability to put things together. As the Near Future it indicated that her life would remain unsettled for some time, without much advancement in her career and in other ways. We see therefore that the defeat of her new self shown as possible might come when that self fails to achieve practical results. The fact that the Tarot has warned her of this stagnant period could help her get through it, as could knowing that it is only the Near Future and not the Outcome.

After the Cross comes the Staff. The first of the four cards, the Six of Cups reversed, lay in the position of Self. And here we found a clearer indication of what had died. The card, when right side up, shows a child in a garden with a larger figure giving her a gift. It implies protection, security, the child whose parents take care of all its needs. Here, however, we see the card reversed. Together with the other cards, especially Death and the Hermit, the image implied that she had overthrown this enclosed, protected way of life. In discussing this card it became clear that in fact the woman had spent most of her life with her parents treating her as their 'little girl'. She had let them do this because of the security it gave her. Even now, as she explained to me, her parents, especially her father, could not accept that she had grown up and must make her own decisions, take her own chances. And of course she herself had found the change hard to accept. Going to law school had been the first step. Before that she had never taken herself seriously enough to do something important. At the same time the school had remained another 'garden' – a situation where she did not have to make any choices, but just follow the strict pattern laid out for her. When the time came for her to take her exam, she had become frightened, and in fact had gone to the therapist to help her pass. The therapy had done this, but it did other things as well. It made her see that she was no longer a child who could let other people make her decisions. The sadness came from this loss.

The next card was in some ways the most important, as well as the simplest in the whole reading. The Three of Cups in the Environment indicated great support from friends. In particular it represented the 'healing circle' and the therapist. Its importance lay in the fact that it showed how much uncritical support she could draw from these people, especially important with the possibility of defeat from a period of stagnancy. The Three of Cups does not show support in any sense of charity or self-sacrifice. The three women dance together. The people around her give her strength simply from being with her, from sharing her experiences and letting *her* support *them*. Notice also the contrast between the Three and the Six. Here the women are all equal; the card carries no sense of sheltering or coddling.

The Three of Cups bears a 'horizontal' connection to the Three of Wands as the Centre. Some of the grounding influences in that image – the figure firmly planted on the hilltop – derive from the support given in the environment. Even though looking back on her life, and exploring new areas, remained essentially lonely activities, she could draw courage from the people around her.

In the position of Hopes and Fears lay one of the more fearful images in the Tarot, the Tower. It signifies destruction, collapse, painful experience. Clearly it represents the woman's fears that all she has accomplished will somehow fly apart. This fear could easily make itself a self-fulfilling prophecy, leading to the Five of Swords reversed, especially without immediate success to reassure and encourage her.

The exaggerated fear goes back to the Six of Cups, and its overthrow. She may have given up a sheltered childlike attitude, she may have been looking on her life with excited expectation, yet a part of her still thought, 'How can I do this? I'm all alone now. I'm not protected any more. I've got to make my own decisions.' And from there it crosses to 'I can't do this. I'm not strong enough, it's all going to fall apart.' When opposition or delay arose, the fear would take over, making it seem like the expected collapse. And the half-conscious thought then becomes 'See? I knew I couldn't do it. Why did I ever cut myself off?' In the reading we discussed the possibility that the Tower also represented a subconscious hope. The subconscious, a very stupid as well as very conservative organ,* will often refuse to accept the loss of a situation it considered safe or secure. No matter that the self knows, even consciously, that it can never return to parental protection. The subconscious does not accept reality. It can easily convince itself that defeat of the current plans will bring a return to safety.

To become aware of such hidden attitudes goes a long way towards overcoming them, for the subconscious depends a great deal on concealment. We can see this by thinking of the times we have harboured some secret anxiety, only to find when we say it out loud that the sheer silliness of the idea dispels it from our mind. A Tarot reading can act in this fashion by identifying the hidden material and showing its probable consequences – in this case, the Five of Swords.

In the position of Outcome lay the Hermit. The first thing to observe about this card is that it does not show success or failure. In contrast with the Three of Wands and the Five of Swords it does not indicate likely practical developments. Instead it points to qualities in the woman herself that in turn will show the way she faces her new situation.

The most obvious meaning of the Hermit derives from its name and basic image. It shows her facing life alone. Now, this does not mean that she loses or denies the support from her environment. If anything, it indicates the need to draw on that support as much as possible. For the Hermit signifies the

---

*Do not confuse the 'subconscious' with the 'unconscious', whose attributes include courage as well as true knowledge. A great deal of confusion has resulted from the use of these two terms as synonymous. I am using the term 'subconscious' here to stand for material – desires, anxieties, fears, hopes – repressed by the conscious mind as it deals with the outer realities of life. 'Unconscious' means the basic energy of life, that area of being beyond the personal ego. The subconscious, despite its hidden qualities, is really an extension of the ego. In a sense, it embodies the ego's absolute domain, that realm where it makes no compromises with reality. Because it does not concern itself with consequences the subsconscious will walk you in front of a truck to avoid an unpleasant conversation. The unconscious, on the other hand, balances and supports us by joining us to the great surge of life beyond our individual selves. The Hanged Man in the Major Arcana gives us a powerful image of this vital connection.

fact that as much as others can help her she alone must make the decisions. Like the figure in the Three of Wands the Hermit stands alone on his mountain.

The Hermit's aloneness, however, does not exist for its own sake. In the Major Arcana it symbolizes the act of withdrawing consciousness from the outer world and events to consider meaning. And of course the idea of meaning fits quite well in this particular reading. To have the Hermit as the Outcome means that the fears, the delays, and the possible defeats do not really matter so much – once the woman accepts her situation. Indeed, the Hermit directly symbolizes psychotherapy.

At the same time the Hermit also hints towards the success of her coming to terms with life. For in its most archetypal aspect it signifies wisdom, true knowledge of the soul gained through removal and introspection. The Hermit's mountain, like the Hanged Man's tree, stands for the conscious mind's connection to the wisdom and life energy of the unconscious.

As the Outcome, therefore, the Hermit indicated that she would understand and accept the changes she had made, half unconsciously, in her life. The mountain symbolism connects the last card to the first, the Three of Wands. The connection, in turn, hints at practical as well as emotional success.

Finally, the Hermit signifies maturity. Through its awareness it carries on the process begun in the Six of Cups reversed, the overthrowing of childlike dependency. It shows her that the situation will resolve itself as the woman overcomes her hesitancy and fears. In the long run the Hermit's mountain stands not for isolation at all, but simply for a quality the woman was only then beginning to experience – self-reliance, confidence in her own ability and judgements.

Because the Outcome showed a working out rather than a result, I decided to turn over another card to get an indication of how events might eventually turn out. The card was another three, the Three of Pentacles. As a card of accomplishment and mastery, it showed the long-term success that was delayed in the Near Future.

THE WORK CYCLE

Despite its power, the Celtic Cross stills works mostly as a descriptive tool, showing us the different influences surrounding some situation. Though it often implies a course of action

('Take a careful approach, work at setting everything up before you do anything' or 'Things won't work out with this person. You'll find your own self again if you let him go.') People sometimes find themselves left with the question, 'What should I do?' While the Tarot does not often give suggestions as concrete as 'Study pottery', or 'Visit your grandmother' it may indicate the sort of action or approach a person needs, leaving the specific details to the individual. As a simple example, the Eight of Pentacles can advise a person 'Keep working at what you are doing. It will take time, but it eventually will bring good results.'

There are other, more subtle, questions that people sometimes ask themselves after a Celtic Cross reading: What if I followed a different set of influences? What if I didn't take this particular attitude to the future, or looked to something different in my past? How would that change the outcome? In other words, what are the possible changes I can make?

To emphasize the possibilities of advice I have devised a new layout for the cards. Based partly on the Celtic Cross and partly on my own arrangement of the Major Arcana, it carries three innovations. First, its whole outlook leans towards advice rather than description. Second, it is open ended; after the reader has reached the last position she or he can lay out more cards, up to ten times the original amount. Of course the reader can do this in any reading, but not in definite positions. The structure of the Work Cycle, as I call this spread, allows the reader to repeat, and keep repeating, the original positions. The effect is to let the reader look at the situation from different sides.

The third innovation involves reading cards in combinations. In many readings (though certainly not all; see the Tree of Life method below) the cards are read individually, even though we attempt to combine the meanings, as in the Cross. In the Work Cycle, however, the positions include the idea of combinations. Readers who know Volume One of this book will remember that my interpretation of the Major Arcana divides the trumps into the Fool plus three lines of seven cards each, with each line showing a different stage of development. They may also remember that each line breaks down further into three parts. The first two cards signify the starting point for the line – the archetypes or basic qualities the person must use in going through the experiences shown in that line. The middle three stand for the basic work of the line -- what the person must assimilate or overcome. The final two cards show the result. Thus, in the first line the Magician and the High Priestess indicate the basic archetypes of life. The Empress, the Emperor, and the Hierophant show the different aspects of the outer world facing us as we grow up. The Lovers and the Chariot symbolize the development of the successful individual. The Work Cycle borrows and adapts this tripartite structure.

THE LAYOUT — POSITIONS AND MEANINGS

The reading begins with choosing the Significator and mixing the cards in the same manner as with the Celtic Cross. Similarly, the first two cards from a small cross, interpreted much the same way as in the older method of reading, with perhaps more emphasis on the crossing card being an outcome or development of the Centre card.

After the small cross the reader turns over seven cards in a row below the Significator rather than around it, with the Significator and Cross standing above the middle card. (See Fig. 61).

This line forms the basic cycle, and the reading may stop with these nine cards. However, if after interpreting this line, the reader and subject desire more information or simply another approach, the reader turns over a second line of seven directly below the first, and so on, until the meaning becomes clear.

In each line the first two cards for the starting point. Their specific meanings derive from the Celtic Cross, the first being Past Experience, interpreted similarly to the Basis card in the older form. The second is Expectations, the person's attitude to the future. In practice, we interpret this card in much the same way as the Hopes and Fears position of the Celtic Cross. Together, the two cards show what has happened and what the person hopes, fears, or simply believes will happen.

The next three cards depart more strongly from the older system. They show what I call the Work — situations, influences, or attitudes the person can use or must overcome. In the Cross the positions represent fairly fixed patterns. This is the way it is. The Work cards indicate possibilities, even opportunities. It emphasizes how the person creates the situation – and can change it.

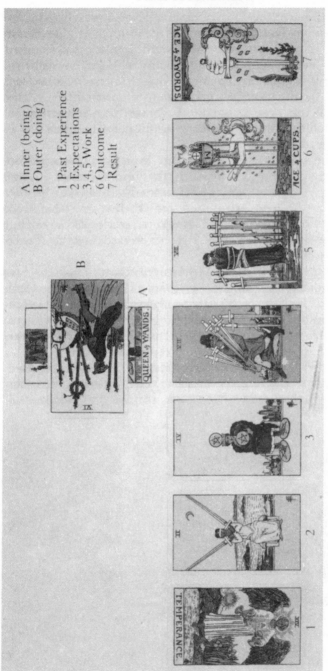

A Inner (being)
B Outer (doing)

1 Past Experience
2 Expectations
3, 4, 5 Work
6 Outcome
7 Result

Figure 61
A sample work cycle pattern

When I began this form of reading I assigned a meaning to each position. The card in the centre indicated Self, the one in the left Others, and the one on the right Events. I soon found it better to give no specific quality to any of them, but rather to interpret them together as simply what the person has to work with in the situation, a combination of possibilities. At the same time the three designations are worth remembering, for one or more of them may help to pinpoint the meaning in specific readings.

Let me give an example of the three as a combination. Suppose a reading deals with that old favourite, a new romance. A woman has met someone she likes but does not know how he feels about her, or whether she should do anything about her feelings. The Work section of the reading shows the Five of Wands, the Hermit reversed, and the Two of Cups (see Fig. 62).

Now, the Two of Cups obviously indicates that the man feels about her in a similar way, just as it would in the Celtic Cross. But here the card further advises the woman to tell the man about her feelings. It also suggests she has much to gain from being with the person, and that the love affair, whether long or short, will affect her life quite strongly.

The Hermit reinforces these ideas. Here its reversed position does not mean immaturity, but rather the idea that now is not the time for aloneness. Instead, the woman will

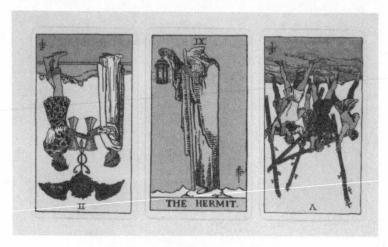

Figure 62

gain most from being involved in the relationship. The Five of Wands, however, suggests that the situation includes conflict. Because it appears right side up, it does not indicate bitterness or even a serious disturbance that the woman should try to avoid. Instead it shows a quickening quality to their fighting, one that exhilarates rather than drains them. And because it occurs in the Work section, it implies she should *use* the energy released through conflict rather than try to avoid it.

The Hermit coming between the two cards indicates perhaps that the woman has spent some time cut off from other people and now wishes (or needs) to return to the world. On the one hand she can use her new relationship to bring her out of herself. On the other hand, she will find involvement with other people brings quarrels and competition, and she must learn to accept and use these things.

Notice that the three cards do not simply show what is, but rather directions and potentials – things to work with. Now let us consider two possible starting points for this imaginary reading and the different ways in which they modify the Work cards. First of all, let us consider the meaning if the first two cards are the Five of Cups and the Three of Cups, connected by the image of the three cups. The first, as Past Experience, indicates the loss of something – most likely the end of a love affair – and would give the background to the Hermit. Therefore, Past Experience tells us that the Hermit stage came as a reaction to an event, but a reaction the woman can now put behind her. The Three reinforces these ideas of new involvement. It shows a very optimistic attitude that will likely carry her over the conflicts that arise.

Suppose, however, that we switch the starting point to Swords, specifically the Eight followed by the Four. The Eight would indicate a history of repression, isolation, confusion, while the Four would suggest that this past situation has left the woman scarred, for as the Expectation it shows a desire to hide from the world, to avoid involvement with others. At the same time the Four would represent a fear – or belief – that she will spend her life alone, with no one breaking into the closed church to awaken her and return her to the world.

With such a starting point the Work cards would indicate an important opportunity for the person. They would tell her that this relationship can bring her out of her lonely Hermit state. The time has come to emerge, and if this emergence brings conflicts and arguments she must accept these too, even use them to involve herself more strongly in life.

The last two positions in the line again feature the idea of combination. As the Outcome and the Result, they go beyond the Celtic Cross's single use of Outcome to sum up the reading. The Outcome indicates the likely way things will develop. The Result, on the other hand, indicates the person's reaction to this development, or the effect it will have on the person's life. This effect can be either experience or attitude. For instance, it can indicate an event or further development that comes about because of the Outcome. The Five of Cups followed by the Eight of Cups would say that the person loses something, or something ends badly, and as a result of this, the person decides to leave, go somewhere new, or start a new phase in life.

Or, the Result card can show the Outcome's effect psychologically. A classic example is the Tower followed by the Star, indicating that an explosion in the person's life would lead to a release of hope and energy. This example also illustrates the potential great importance of seeing not just the Outcome, but what comes afterwards. If a reading showed only the Tower, and not the Star as a result of it, it would leave the subject with a sense of devastation.

Very often the first line will give such a strong picture that the person will need no further information. At other times, however, the line may leave the person slightly confused, or simply wishing to see the situation from a different point of view. In this case, the reader may simply turn over another line directly under the first. The positions remain the same, and the seven cards still relate to the original small cross that set out the basic situation. And yet, because we begin with a different starting point, the line enables us to see the situation in a different way.

Besides the new information gained, this method helps answer a question many people ask about Tarot readings: 'If I did it again, different cards would appear, so how can these cards really mean anything? The answer is that the new cards will look at the same situation from a new point of view.

Very often, if a reader sets out a Celtic Cross, then mixes the cards and does it over again, many of the same or similar cards will appear in the second reading. In one pair of readings I did for a married couple (with someone else's reading in between) six out of the ten cards were the same, and the Environment card in the woman's reading was the one used as the Significator for the man. The Work Cycle, because it actually prevents the same cards from appearing, tends more to show different sides to the question.

Sometimes the second line will almost mirror the first, indicating that the situation is heading so strongly in this direction that the person will not easily change it. At other times, however, the Outcome-Result will show a definite alternative to the first line, and then the reader must look to the starting points and to the Work cards.

A SAMPLE READING

Once I did a reading for a woman with a jealous lover. Theoretically the two did not expect each other to be monogamous but the woman knew that if she went with someone else – and someone else had come along – her lover would be upset. She wanted advice on what to do and we did a Work Cycle (see Fig. 63).

Before the reading I remarked to the woman that the Three of Cups often appears in such situations, right side up if it is going well, reversed if it is not. The reading began with the Three of Cups reversed crossed by the Ace of Cups. The combination showed that despite the jealousies and arguments the situation was giving her a lot of happiness, if only she could work it out. The first line then began very positively with the Ace of Pentacles as the Past, and the Sun as a highly optimistic Expectation for the future. Now, the Ace of Pentacles, besides showing happiness and pleasure, also carries a sense of security, of protected and enclosed situations. For some time the woman and her lover had not related much to other people, building up a tight emotional 'garden' around themselves as the Ace symbolism shows (they were, in fact, living in a remote house in the Welsh countryside).

The Sun shows the child riding out of a garden. The woman hoped now to break loose into wider experiences. And, since the Ace of Pentacles had changed in the present to the Ace of Cups, at least as a possibility, the cards showed that she had begun to let loose, to pour out her emotions regardless of security.

The Work seemed even more to suggest freedom. The Star, the Tower, and the World, all trumps from the last line,

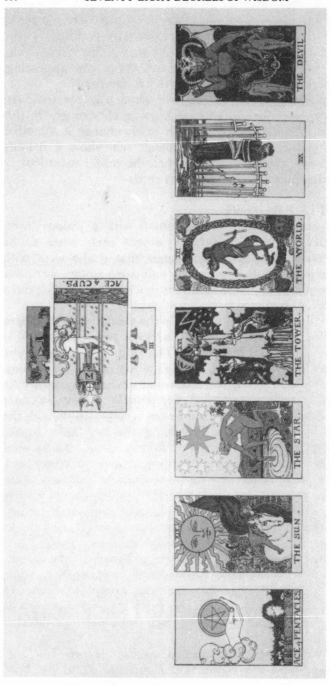

Figure 63(a)
A sample work cycle reading

showed first of all the power of the situation. In the centre the Tower symbolized the stormy battles and overpowering emotions involved. It also suggested the danger of her secure relationship being broken down by the lightning bolts of jealousy and resentment. Now, the Star here did not particularly indicate a release coming after the Tower, as it would at the end of the line. Rather, it told her that in this difficult situation she needed optimism and extreme openness about her own desires and emotions. The World also indicated optimism, implying the possibility of combining the opposing goals of a firm relationship and freedom.

And yet, despite all these positive infiuences, the end cards looked very unpromising. The Eight of Swords followed by the Devil implied that she would make an attempt to break loose from the confining qualities of her situation. The Result, however, showed she would probably fail to get free. The happy and comfortable security of the Ace of Pentacles had become changed to Devil-like repression, with her and her original lover chained to a situation that neither of them really wanted.

To try for another viewpoint – and also to understand what went wrong in the first line – we laid down a second row (see Fig. 63(b)).

This line began more soberly. The Past Experience showed the Seven of Swords, indicating half-hearted attempts to break out of the confinement in her life. It implied that previously she had never seriously pushed the question or faced the real problems involved. This card alone hinted at the reasons for the Devil asserting itself – the woman had never tried to work out what had to be done, had never confronted her lover or the problems between them.

The second card carried this idea further. Justice showed not just a hope for everyone to be 'fair' rather than repressive or selfish, but even more, a desire to see everything clearly and face the truth about herself – what *she* had done with her life, as well as dealing with the reactions of the others. A harsher, much tougher attitude than the Sun, Justice symbolized a commitment to reality, to creating a real future for herself. Notice that the Sun shows a free child, without responsibilities – the opposite of Justice.

The Work in this line – the Nine of Cups, the Four of Pentacles, the Wheel reversed – continued the theme of

Figure 63 (b)
A sample work cycle reading continued

realism. The Nine of Cups showed a need to balance the emotional pressure with light enjoyment. On the other side the Wheel reversed indicated being able to sort through all the illusions involved. It showed as well the need to gain control of the situation, to refuse to allow the Wheel of events to simply spin her along whichever way it turned. Justice became then not just a hope but the primary method of moving away from passiveness and subjectivity.

Of the three cards in the middle, the Four of Pentacles proved the most interesting, especially compared with the Tower above it. Where the trump had shown her flying apart under the impact of everyone's charged emotions the Four of Pentacles showed her protecting herself. It showed her holding on to her own needs, her own understanding of the situation, despite the pressure on her from her two lovers. The two cards around it indicated ways to do this; first by enjoying herself and using that pleasure to hold herself together; and second by understanding what had happened and why it had happened. The Wheel reversed on the right indicated the need – and the opportunity – actually to apply her hope for Justice, that is, to work hard at understanding the true meaning of all the changes going on in her life.

In discussing these two lines the woman said that the first looked to her like what she *should* want, and the second what she really wanted. People around her talked so much of 'freedom' and open relationships without painful consequences that she felt pressured to want this 'Sun' kind of behaviour. In reality she cared much more for Justice, the truth. The result of the second line's harsher, more realistic starting point showed the sense of what she said. The Outcome card was the Queen of Wands, with the Six of Wands as the Result. The Queen indicated that by looking first to Justice rather than an overly optimistic Sun, the woman would find a sense of her own strength and joy. She would become more dependent on herself rather than the outside situation. From this would come the confidence and belief of the Six, an optimism which would carry the other people along with her.

THE TREE OF LIFE

Any Tarot reading originates in a particular moment; by

describing the influences and trends it reaches to past and future. The shorter forms tend only to reach far enough to illuminate some particular situation. When we begin to know the cards better, we may look for some method to give a wider picture of a person's place in the world. The Tree of Life reading, which uses the whole deck and is similar in scope to a natal astrology chart (though perhaps more narrowly focussed on the spiritual/psychological), provides this fuller understanding.

The image of the Tree comes from the Qabalah. We can see it in the Rider pack on the Ten of Pentacles, drawn in the following way:

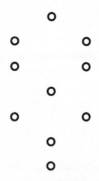

In meditation with the Major Arcana, we use primarily the twenty-two positions or links between the different Sephiroth (the ten positions). In divination we use the Sephiroth themselves, adapting their classical names and connotations to enable them to serve as positions in a spread, similar to the Basis, Self, etc. of a Celtic Cross, but much wider in scope. The Qabalist titles and descriptions are necessarily abstract; they contain a mystic description of the universe's creation and structure, as well as a way towards a greater knowledge of God. Therefore those Tarot readers like myself, who have wished to use this powerful image for divination have chosen more mundane meanings to correspond to the positions.

THE STRUCTURE OF THE TREE

Before going through these meanings, we should look briefly at the Tree's structure. There are two basic patterns within the Tree, shown as follows:

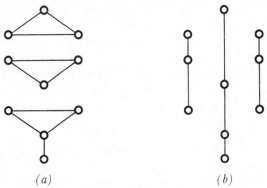

(a)   (b)

Diagram (a) emphasizes levels of awareness. The top triangle remains closest to God, from whom the original point of light emanated to create the first Sephirah. As the light of creation travelled through the different triangles it became more and more diluted, or even for some people corrupted, until in the last, single, Sephirah it became contained within the physical world of flesh and rock and water. (Such a brief description of course greatly distorts Qabalist philosophy. I give it here only to show something of the background for the Tree of Life reading.)

The concept of a downward descent of the light is used in divination in the following way. Since we wish to describe a person's life we look at each triangle as an aspect of that person, using a tripartite system similar to the three lines of the Major Arcana. The top triangle signifies a person's spiritual existence, pointing upwards to the subject's highest potential. The middle triangle pointing downwards to manifestation, represents the ways in which the person deals with the outer world, the practical matters of life. The bottom triangle again points downwards but this time into the hidden areas of the self. It stands for unconscious drives and imaginative energy. We can also refer to the triangles as super-conscious, conscious- and unconscious.

The bottom position, standing apart, represents not a personal quality as do the others, but the outer world in which the person lives. We can think of it as similar to Environment in the Celtic Cross, but on a much wider level.

Diagram (b) derives from the idea of polarity or opposing forces. In Qabalah the right and left sides of the Tree signify the way in which God directs existence. The right pillar, that

of Grace, tends towards expansion. Its qualities enlarge and
open out. The left pillar, called Severity, contracts, emphasizing qualities that restrict. The one gives, the other takes away,
thereby maintaining the conservation of energy. But if only
those two forces existed the universe would swing wildly back
and forth, constantly expanding and contracting. Therefore,
the middle pillar stands for Reconciliation, a blending and
harmonizing of the two principles. Notice that the last
Sephirah, symbolizing physical existence, falls in the middle
pillar. In the material world the archetypal elements merge
into a stable form.

The image of the three columns appears in less abstract
form in the Rider pack version (as well as a number of others)
of the High Priestess. The dark pillar stands for Severity, the
light pillar for Grace. The High Priestess herself fulfils the
function of Reconciliation, balancing the yin and yang
opposites within perfect stillness.

Just as we need a 'practical' version of the triangles, so our
purpose requires a more diredt interpretation of the three
pillars. We therefore use a recurring pattern for each triangle.
The position on the left tends towards the problems arising
from that level, the one on the right depicts the benefits or
positive direction. The position in the middle describes the
quality itself, where the oppositions are blended together.
These distinctions will become clearer when we look at the
individual Sephiroth.

One further point about the structure. Qabalists picture the
path made by the light of creation as a zigzag, sometimes
referred to as the lightning bolt of God. Beginning beyond the
first Sephirah (for God's true essence remains unknowable
and transcendent) it runs like this:

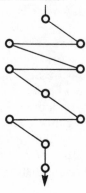

In meditation we use this image primarily to help us advance through the Sephiroth towards union with that aspect of God we experience in mystic ecstasy. In other words, through meditative discipline we travel backwards along the lightning bolt, as if we were unravelling the universe to get to its source. The lightning striking the Tower in the Major Arcana symbolizes this light of illumination.

Another form of meditation, mixed with ceremonial magic, attempts to follow the lightning downwards, or rather to call it down upon the person. Called 'Practical Qabalah', this use of Qabalistic principles for magic bases much of its work on the idea that proper ritual and meditation can bring a lightning flash, not just of understanding, but of great power onto the magician. The person following these occult practices is warned not to seek this power for personal gain but only for projects serving the community. (The warnings against misuse given in magical grimoires sometimes strike one as similar to the warnings on pornographic books: 'This material is for medical use only'.)

THE LAYOUT

In divination we follow the lightning pattern in a much more mundane way, as the method of laying out the cards. To do a Tree of Life reading the reader first removes the Significator as in the other methods, and places it high on the reading surface (obviously a lot of room is needed to lay out seventy-eight cards). When the subject has shuffled and cut the deck, the reader takes the cards and begins laying them face down according to the pattern:

```
                    1


        3                    2


        5                    4


                 6


        8                    7


                 9


                10
```

The Significator remains exposed above the reading. When the first ten cards are placed the reader lays down another ten on top of them, and so on, until each place contains a pack of seven cards. Now, removing the Significator from the deck leaves seventy-seven cards, or eleven times seven. Therefore, the reader will end up with seven extra cards. Many Qabalists speak of an 'invisible' eleventh Sephirah, known as Daath, or Knowledge. Usually Qabalists will place this extra Sephirah in the middle pillar, between the first and sixth Sephiroth, that is, between the top and middle triangles. In Tarot readings we place it to the side or on the bottom, and read it after all the others. The fact that we do not place it down in order with the other cards but simply use the 'left over' seven cards emphasizes its uniqueness. The Daath pack does not belong in any of the general areas of influence. Some readers see it as signifying the immediate future.

When I first began doing the Tree of Life readings I used the Daath pack as a general commentary, an extra bit of information applying to the reading as a whole. I have since found a more specific meaning for it, that of Transformation.

In Volume One I described the idea, derived both from Qabalah and modern quantum mechanics, that any change comes not as gradual alteration, but as a jump from one state to another. We may lead up to changes with years of gradual preparation but the actual change occurs as a leap across an abyss. We cease being one thing and become another. In these moments of transformation we can sometimes sense the essential Nothing underlying all fixed existence. Some people describe Daath as the aspect which sense this truth of the abyss. Others point out that Daath links Wisdom (Sephirah 2) and Understanding (Sephirah 3) through its qualities of awareness and reflection. Indeeed, 'Daath' means 'Knowledge'.

With these meanings in mind I found it worthwhile to use the Daath pack as a description of the means by which a person changes. Related to the whole reading it emphasizes the connections a person makes between the different levels. The different Sephiroth/positions tend to show distinct levels and conditions of being. The Daath pack helps us see how we move between them. Therefore, the name I have given it is Transformation.

THE POSITIONS AND MEANINGS

What then are the specific Sephiroth positions? The following list is my own, based partly on suggestions from various commentaries. I offer it as a possible system and a guide. Readers who want to work extensively with Tree of Life divination will want to formulate their own positions.

Using the number pattern shown on p.173, the positions are:

1 Kether or Crown – Highest Spiritual Development

By this we mean the truest and best qualities of the person and the ways in which she or he reaches these levels. The Crown will not always show very positive or joyous qualities. Some people reach their best development through struggle or sadness. I remember one reading where the Tower occupied the centre of the Kether line, with the Star two cards away from it. The person found it very difficult to develop in any stable way. He tended always to go through cycles of tension, explosion, and release, a theme echoed all the way at the bottom of the reading, when the Devil appeared in the centre of his Daath line.

2 Hokmah or Wisdom

The second Sephirah, Hokmah or Wisdom, stands for Creative Intelligence, the ways in which the person moves towards the goal of Highest Development. Usually related to the Crown line it emphasizes the process of development rather than the result. For example, if the Sun appears in the Crown line we would interpret it as joy and freedom, appreciated for themselves. If it appeared in Creative Intelligence we would think of those qualities as the means towards whatever we had seen in the Crown. Like the first line, Creative Intelligence may include unpleasant or difficult cards, if these are what the person uses to grow.

When such cards do appear it is important to consider them not only in relation to their function – to see how the person can use them creatively – but also in relation to the other cards in the line. For example, suppose the Nine of Wands appeared in Hokmah. The reader would first emphasize the strength and determination rather than the rigidity inherent in the card. But suppose the Four of Wands appeared in the line as well. Then the Nine has to be seen as part of a cycle of defence and openness, each of them helping and feeding on each other.

And because they appear in the second line of the Spirit triangle, we would think of them not simply as a cycle repeating the same experience over and over, but as a spiral, leading to whatever images appeared in Kether.

It should become obvious that the Tree of Life reading requires a good deal of experience with the cards and with divination to work properly. Not only must the reader interpret seven cards for every position, but each position must relate to the others.

3 Binah or Understanding

Completing the triangle is Binah, Understanding. In Qabalah the difference between Wisdom and Understanding refers primarily to the manner in which the soul contemplates God and itself. In the more mundane experience of a reading we can think of Understanding as those experiences which hold us back from development, or Sorrows and Burdens. Here the cards show the person's restrictions and this time the more positive images need to be adapted to the terms of the line. At the same time the original title, Understanding, leads us to consider how these restrictions can be overcome.

The middle triangle stands for the more ordinary aspects of life, and here we begin with the two sides and end in the middle.

4 Gevurah or Judgement

Opposite Worldly Gains we find Gevurah, or Judgement, standing for Difficulties. These may include anything from money troubles to loneliness. In one reading the Queen of Swords in this line indicated to me that the woman was a widow.

5 Hesed or Mercy

The fifth Sephirah stands for Worldly Gains, which means what the person will achieve in life in terms of work, home, money, friends, etc. Usually the line will emphasize areas of success rather than failure. It may also indicate the ways in which worldly gains affect the person's character. The three triangles form one pattern, a fact that usually becomes more and more apparent as the reading develops and connections appear more strongly. Therefore, the mundane concerns of Worldly Gains will often reflect the spiritual awareness of

Creative Force above it. And understanding the lower positions on the Tree will often prove the key to going back and
interpreting the higher ones.

6 Tifereth or Beauty

The point of the triangle stands for Tifereth, Beauty. In
readings I use this position to indicate Health. Using the
Tarot to diagnose specific physical problems can be a very
tricky operation, though suggestions for doing this exist,
usually linking the cards to astrological aspects or other
systems. I have found it better to get a more general picture
from the line, looking not just at physical condition but also
emotional, spiritual health.

One recommendation – observe which elements dominate.
Strong Wands suggest good general health through the
person's life, though of course such Wands as the Ten or the
Nine, as well as reversed Wands, might indicate the opposite.
Cups and Swords tend to show the emotional and spiritual
condition of the person, while Pentacles often show weaker
health or the need to take care of the body. The Five, for
instance, would be a definite warning. A predominance of
Major cards in the line is more difficult to interpret, depending for meaning on which cards appear. Strength, of course,
would indicate good general health, Temperance would
indicate illness averted by caution, while the Devil might show
sickness, or hypochondria. Sometimes a single Major card can
symbolize some special situation that has appeared or will
appear in the person's life. Time sequences in this line, and in
the whole tree, remain a difficult problem, especially for the
beginning reader.

The third triangle deals with the Unconscious, particularly
the imaginative and sexual drives. In Volume One we looked
at the idea that super-consciousness, or spiritual energy and
awareness, consists of the unconscious transformed and made
conscious. Thus, the Tree will often show very strong connections between the top and bottom triangles, with the middle
level – the person's conscious experiences – forming a link
between the two.

Earlier I described the subconscious as the repressed side of
the ego, distinct from the unconscious, or life energy of the
person. None of these triangles deals specifically with this
sense of the subconscious. Rather, this hidden material can

appear throughout the reading, showing problems, aggression, or unfulfilled desires. Unfortunately the vastness of this subject prevents me giving detailed examples. (I apologize for indulging in something resembling the dark hints one often finds in occult books: 'Here I may say no more about this.') I will only point out that we can see the subconscious at work in the seeming contradictions of, say, the Two of Swords appearing as a block in the line of Creative Force.

7 Netzach or Eternity

The seventh Sephirah, Netzach, means Eternity. I have used it in this system to stand for Discipline, the ways in which the person can put her or his imagination to work. By 'discipline' I do not mean the strict sort of rules that the word normally conjures up. Instead I mean the deliberate training and direction symbolized in the hooded hawk of the Nine of Pentacles. Creative power under such discipline becomes enhanced and freed rather than weakened or closed in. For it is a quality of the unconscious that its benefit in our lives increases the more we direct it. This is something known by most artists, as well as by people who have worked seriously in the occult.

Most people who do not deliberately work with the unconscious energy simply find that it stays dormant. Their lives may seem flat, or they may think of themselves as lacking any creativity. For some, however, the unconscious is so strong it can break through on its own, bringing chaos or even madness. I remember one reading (not a Tree of Life) done for a man who had experienced a serious nervous breakdown after a series of strong psychic experiences. In the reading the Nine of Pentacles appeared, but also the Hermit, telling him that a proper teacher would train this energy that had erupted so painfully into his life. Discipline, in its best sense, stands for the process of raising the unconscious and transforming it into creative energy.

Because most people do not find themselves drawn, or pushed, to psychic or occult work, we usually find more ordinary concerns reflected in Discipline. It may refer to artistic work, but not necessarily. For some people, the unconscious expresses itself in a career or in creating a loving home for her or his family. The important thing about the line is that it shows the training or work necessary for the person to do something with creative potential. Such blocked cards as the Eight of Swords appearing in this line may hold great meaning for the entire reading, for so much of our lives depends on the release of unconscious energy.

8 Hod or Reverberation

On the other side of the triangle we find Hod, or Reverberation. The divination title for this line – Love and Lust – will usually make the subject sit up and listen very closely. This line shows the person's sexual drive and the way these urges work in practice – in short, what the person wants and what he or she gets. Depending on the person this line too may provide the key to all the others, though maybe not as often as we might expect.

Notice that Love and Lust comes on the restrictive side of the Tree, while Discipline appears on the side of expansion. This construction reflects the fact that our sexual drives often dominate us, making us do things we would otherwise avoid, or preventing us from releasing potentials in other areas. Discipline, on the other hand, makes use of the imaginative energy, leading it in the direction of transformation to the spiritual. Sexual cards may appear not in Love and Lust but in Discipline, suggesting that the person develops through love, in the manner symbolized by the angel rising between the man and woman in the Lovers. For such people love is as much a discipline as a temptation or an indulgence.

I should add that Love and Lust appearing on the side of Restriction does not require us to interpret it as a problem. If the cards show satisfaction and freedom, then certainly we should interpret them that way.

9 Yesod or Foundation

The ninth Sephirah, Yesod or Foundation, stands for Imagination, in many ways the true foundation of the self. For the majority of people, who do not go through programmes of self-creation the unconscious never does become conscious. It remains both the source and the driving force of the personality. We glimpse this energy in such activities as dreams, fantasies, desires – in other words, what we commonly call the imagination. By calling the Foundation line Imagination we actually mean more than such manifestations. The term here stands for the energy itself, coiled beneath the conscious personality and giving off flashes to the outer world. The cards in

this line show the shape and mood of the person's unconscious. Often they will relate very directly to the line of
Highest Development way above it.

10 Malkuth or Kingdom

Below Imagination comes Malkuth, or Kingdom, meaning the
World around the person. Here we see the external influences,
other people, situations both personal and social/political.
Usually, of course, indications of these outside forces will
appear throughout the reading. In one reading the Emperor,
as the woman's domineering husband, appeared in the centre
of her Health line, that is, in the exact centre of the Tree.
However, the last line emphasizes outer influences, showing
also the effect upon the subject. We can look at it as similar to
the Environment of the Cross, but greatly expanded.

Daath

Finally we come to Daath. Though we set it aside from the
Tree when dealing out the cards, many readers will want to
lay it out below Malkuth, thereby producing a symmetrical
Tree as well as graphically showing how connections underlie
all positions.

Sometimes these cards will clearly refer to one particular
situation shown above in one of the three triangles. Usually,
we do not give the Daath cards a specific function as we do
with the other lines. Like the Fool in the Major Arcana, it
moves between all of them, joining things together, helping
the general pattern become clearer in the reader's and subject's minds.

The image of the entire Tree, seventy-eight brightly
coloured cards, can be an astounding sight. I have sometimes
taken photographs of it for myself and for the subject. I would
recommend readers to make a chart of the Tree, marking the
positions and the individual cards. Most people also find it
valuable to make a cassette recording which they can play
back later to help assimilate the tremendous amount of information.

If the reader and the subject have begun a regular
programme of readings, then a Tree of Life, written and
recorded, can help make the readings more effective. Often it
works best not to do the Tree immediately, but rather to do
one or two small readings first to get an idea of the issues in

the person's life. A Tree of Life will then provide a comprehensive view of the subject, which both people can use as a reference in later readings.

To do such a reading requires a great knowledge of the cards and of the ways in which they mesh together. Remember that the astrologer doing a natal chart is usually able to construct the chart ahead of time and consider its various qualities before having to explain it to the subject. But a Tree of Life reading, like any Tarot reading, works best when we interpret the cards as we lay them out.

Remember also that each line contains seven cards. Each line is itself a reading. Sometimes the seven cards appear as a group of individual experiences. More often, a pattern will form within the line. Our understanding of it may move from, say, left to right almost like a story; or we might focus on the centre card as a dominant theme, with the surrounding cards interpreted partly according to their positions. I have often found symmetry an important clue – cards one and seven relating to each other, two and six, etc. Or, the three cards on the right may show one characteristic, while the ones on the left some other, possibly contradictory one. Each line carries its own movement, its own perfection.

Chapter 7.

How to Use Tarot Readings

The value of a Tarot reading, at least for the subject, depends on what he or she does with it afterwards. For those people who come to a reader out of curiosity or as a game the reading will probably pass by their lives, like a show they watch from the audience. But this show concerns them, and if the reading means anything real, they will want to put it to some practical use.

First of all, the reader and the subject cannot use the reading at all until they understand it. Therefore the reader must develop skills of interpretation, and the best way to do this is to practise. When you begin do not assume a great depth of knowledge; just keep at it. Do not worry if you cannot see how things fit together, or become confused by all the possible interpretations of some single card. After a while you will find that you notice things that would have slid past you when you first began.

Study. Learn the meanings described in whatever books strike you as valuable. Then begin the process of making your own book. Get a good notebook and record your descriptions, feelings, and experiences for each card. You can do this in words, pictures, diagrams, whatever method means something to you. In the same or another book record the readings you do and what you have learned from them. If some reading teaches you a new point about some single card or combination or the whole deck, record this as well.

Do not take for granted that you know what you have already learned. We all carry certain biases and as time goes by we tend to remember some meanings and forget others. Often a card will make no sense because we insist on interpreting it in a certain way strictly from habit, when another, forgotten meaning will clear it immediately. Therefore, from time to time, even after you think you know all the cards by heart, look back on your notes and your books. You will be surprised at how much you relearn.

Keeping a notebook serves another purpose. As described above Tarot readings help teach us a balance between intuition and action, the High Priestess and the Magician. A notebook is one practical way to develop this balance, for it combines your own impressions with the ideas you have learned from published texts. Making your own book is especially important if you are the sort of person who believes what you learn from a published book or a teacher. You are the reader, and in any situation the cards lie before you and no one else. Without the ability to respond instinctively to the pictures you will never be able to choose between the possible interpretations, let alone find a new meaning just right for that reading.

We all possess the ability to respond intuitively, but like any other faculty, this kind of perception requires training and development. A notebook will help here too. Besides giving you something permanent to look at later, the very act of writing them down will give your ideas more substance. You will also find the original ideas will be greatly extended as new points occur to you while you write them down.

You can also train the intuition by spending time with the pictures, looking at them, mixing them, telling stories with them, above all, forgetting what they are *supposed* to mean. Forget the symbolism as you pay attention to the colours, the shapes, the very feel and weight of the cards.

As the reader becomes more competent the readings will become more valuable. The primary thing we get from any reading is information, but the information can be of different kinds. For people with an awareness of the spiritual undercurrents shaping all our lives the Tarot can show what particular shape these currents are taking at that moment. For others, readings may show the likely developments from some particular situation or decision. Look for a new job, start a love affair, continue writing a novel – these are all mundane issues, seemingly far from the mystic concerns of the Major Arcana. Nevertheless, these are the things most people look at in Tarot readings; and in fact they are also the ways in which we truly develop, because they are the ways we involve ourselves in life.

They form the reality rising out of the spiritual undercurrents. A Tarot reading can help us examine the consequences of such actions and decisions.

Tarot readings, then, can give us information. But to act on that information, especially if it goes against our desires, remains very difficult.

We can think up endless dodges to deny the validity of Tarot readings. On one level we tell ourselves, 'It's only a pack of cards.' But even those who do not dismiss the Tarot's predictions so easily may think, 'Now that I know what it says I can make sure it won't work out that way.' Around the time I first began to use Tarot cards I consulted them on something I wanted to do but recognized was dangerous. The cards indicated disaster and spelled out quite clear the shape that disaster would take. I then said to myself, 'Well, now that I've seen the dangers I can make sure I avoid them.' I went ahead with what I wanted to do, and the situation worked out, in detail, the way the cards had predicted. Not having learned my lesson I read the cards again, hoping not for the truth, but for some reassuring message. I was using a book of meanings at that time, and when I looked up the Basis card the book gave as an interpretation, 'Failure to follow good advice'.

The problem with making a decision based on a Tarot reading is that we never know how it would have turned out otherwise. Suppose a student considers leaving college and the cards advise strongly against it. If she follows the reading she will never know what might have happened if she had followed her desire instead. Of course the whole point of the reading is that it does tell her what would have happened. But, she will always wonder, suppose it was not true? A prediction, especially from a pack of cards, can never carry the same impact as actual experience. Curiosity alone can make us do disastrous things.

It takes courage to overcome curiosity and desire. Some years ago I read that the poet Allen Ginsberg and a woman lover of his were thinking of having a baby together. They did a reading, with the Tarot or the I Ching, I forget which, and got a negative prediction. They gave up the idea. I do not know how much they really wanted a child, but I remember admiring their strength in resisting the desire. I once did not go to a potentially valuable conference because the cards showed me unpleasant consequences. I was able to recognize the truth of what the cards indicated, at least in regard to what I would have contributed to the situation. Even so, I found it difficult not to ignore the information and go ahead.

We can think up some truly marvellous excuses for avoiding the obvious truth of a reading. If we respect the cards too much to simply declare them nonsense, we will often look for certain 'false' images to discredit the whole reading. Does the Outcome card not seem to fit the situation? Rather than interpret it in the light of the others, we will write off the whole reading.

Some books advise readers never to read for themselves because of the lack of objectivity. For a long time I went to a friend for readings and she to me, because neither of us trusted ourselves to interpret our own cards honestly. When I started doing my own readings I still found it hard to overcome various mental tricks to avoid unpleasant images. My favourite worked as follows: I could not ignore the cards I did not like or simply declare them untrue or exaggerated. That would have seemed too obvious. Therefore I looked in the reading for some very positive image, such as the Ace of Cups, and said to myself, 'Well, that can't be true, nothing so good could come out of this mess.' And then I would dismiss the whole reading on the grounds that if this one card made no sense none of the others did. Another trick I discovered myself doing was to lay out the cards very casually, so if something bad came up I could think, 'Well, I didn't really mean it, I didn't do it seriously.' I could only read for myself when I began treating the readings in the same way I would anyone else's, mixing the cards carefully, working at the images, trying to get some direction for action (or inaction).

A reading will not always give a clear yes or no answer to a question. It may show simply a complex of trends and influences. Sometimes the reading does not involve a choice because of an ongoing situation which cannot easily be avoided. Then specific images and meanings become very important. The Tarot can help us pinpoint the important elements in the situation, the ones that need the most work to change, or bring about, the predicted outcome.

People may use the idea, 'Now that I know what it says, I can do something about it' as an excuse to follow their desires. Nevertheless, the statement remains true. Maybe we have a very pessimistic attitude or an exaggerated fear, or an unreasonable hope. To recognize such things helps us gain a clearer perspective. Maybe our past experience governs our behaviour or confuses what we expect from the future. Knowing this consciously can put us on the way to overcoming it. Or maybe the cards will show us someone else's jealousy or vindictiveness; we can then take steps to free ourselves from that person's influence. Or, if the cards show love and support from someone, we know we can trust that person.

All these things require some sort of response to make them real. We cannot expect to make use of a person's friendship if we do not make ourselves open to it. Wherever possible the reader should try to point out to the subject definite steps which can be taken to make best use of the information. If the reader cannot recommend a concrete course of action then he or she should point out what area the subject needs to work on.

Above all, the reader must learn to form a coherent pattern from the reading. Often, beginning readers will learn the cards and advance to the point where they can skilfully interpret each image in its specific position. At the end the subject finds him or herself with a jumble of different points and no clear idea of how it all fits together. A good reader can sum up what the reading says in a few sentences. Usually I will try to do this at both the beginning and end of the reading, impressing on the subject's mind the most important points. Does the Environment support or hinder? Do the person's Expectations help or hurt? Will the Outcome bring a valuable Result? The subject needs these questions answered, not just in all their complexity, but also in as simple a way as possible. And how does one thing come out of another? How does the past help form the future? What does the person contribute to the overall situation?

Along with coherency comes the need for a positive approach. It is not enough to depict things as they are. The person wants to know what to do, what not to do. If the cards show something good, the subject still needs to know how to help this along. And if they show disaster the reader must say so, but can also say what, if anything, the person can do. What brings about this unpleasant Outcome? Can these influences be altered or avoided? How can the person counteract, or at least cushion it? What elements show other possibilities? Can we look for anything good to come out of it?

If the Outcome arises from some particular course of action, should the person abandon it? When we do a Tarot reading for someone we take on the responsibility of trying to send that person in a positive direction.

Beyond specific suggestions of do this rather than that, lies a wider area of possible action derived from the ways the suits balance each other. In the introduction to each suit we considered its problems and the way we could 'add' other suits/ elements. In practice, this adding is often difficult to achieve, because it means breaking the pattern shown in the reading itself. For this very reason, however, it is worth trying in situations where the reading shows a dead end if the person stays with the elements given.

The most direct way to bring in an outside influence involves simple suggestions. If the reading indicates a need for the grounding influence of Pentacles, the subject can try doing more physical things, such as sports or gardening, or paying more attention to more mundane activities, such as work or study or keeping busy around the house. If the reading shows a need for the watery qualities of Cups, then the reader may emphasize the person's dreams and fantasies, and may suggest activities such as meditation or drawing. A person can fill a need for Wands by becoming more active physically, competing with other people, or starting new projects. And a need for Swords would call for a sober, carefully thought out approach to the person's situation. The important thing about these recommendations is that they reach beyond the reading. They deal with the cards that do not appear as well as the ones that do. Therefore, beginning readers should use this method carefully, lest they assume too much knowledge and control on their part.

MEDITATION

So far, we have considered practical responses to the information gained from a reading. But a Tarot reading is not the words describing it; it is rather a series of pictures. And the most direct response to a reading depends on working with the pictures themselves. For people who know the cards well, or for people with some experience in meditation, it becomes possible to work directly with the images to help bring about the effects associated with that card. There is nothing vague or mysterious about this process. It requires concentration as well as instinctive feeling, and it does not replace practical steps. On the contrary, it helps to make those steps more accessible. For if the card Strength appears in a reading as something we need in our life, why not let the card itself help give it to us?

Besides actual meditation I often recommend to people that they carry a certain card around with them, and try to remain conscious of it being there, taking it out from time to time, looking at it, thinking about what it means. The constant awareness helps keep the entire reading in focus as well.

Meditation can also help to bring in new influences from outside the reading. Suppose the Star does not appear in the reading, but as the reader we think it *should*. In other words, the archetype of the Star seems to us to symbolize exactly those qualities the person needs. Now, we can show the person the card and discuss the ideas associated with it. It is more valuable, however, to give the person an actual experience of the card.

Briefly, the method works as follows. We begin by leading the person into a meditative state; help him or her to relax, to breathe deeply, to release all the thoughts and tensions cluttering up consciousness. When the subject has reached this level (and with a little experience we can sense this), we then begin to give suggestions leading into the card. The suggestions may be a description of the card to set the scene (with the Empress, for example, 'You are in a garden full of flowers, with a river running alongside it. There is a woman lying on a couch ...') or more simply, basic images such as sun, water, wind, that belong to the card's archetypal qualities.

Usually it is best to keep these opening suggestions as simple as possible. If we describe the card we should not try to include all the details. Let the subject create the actual impressions. We function only as a guide to urge the person along.

We can keep the experience on this basic level or we can develop it further. We can give more complex suggestions, and start asking questions – 'What do you see?' 'What is the person doing?' 'Can you hear anything?' – so that the subject begins to extend the fantasy beyond our directions. Sometimes the meditation will allow the person to experience the archetypal elements in a new way. At other times it may go even further; the images will transform themselves, releasing some intense awareness from inside the person. A number of times I have led a group meditation with a class, and afterwards have had someone tell me that the meditation has allowed him or her to resolve some longstanding problem or emotional block. Such breakthroughs, of course, came from the people themselves. They were ready to go beyond their current state to a new level, had been ready for some time, but could not bring themselves to cross over. The meditation allowed them to do this without realizing it until it had happened.

Meditation can also help a person develop a deeper and more personal sense of some particular card. Once, I did a meditation with someone who found the Emperor a hard remote image, almost frightening, and certainly unattractive. I began by setting the scene for her – a stony desert by a narrow image. This then opened out to a vast plain filled with the Emperor's subjects. When I pushed her to describe these people she saw them all hooded – that is, faceless – and bent over, working on robot-like tasks. The Emperor's fierce expression kept the people from daring to look at him. The people symbolized the woman, and her unwillingness to go more deeply into the card.

I then told the woman to do just that – not just look at the Emperor but go right up to him. When her fantasy-self did this a strange thing happened. The Emperor changed from a despot to a kind of harmless puppet, while from behind him rose a vast ghost or spirit figure, beautiful and benevolent. The woman's fear and reaction against the social structure of the Emperor had given way to a sense of the spiritual structure underlying the universe.

This experience not only gave the *woman* a much greater sense of the Emperor's deeper significance; it had the same effect on me. With her I went beyond the image of the Emperor as society to the more occult meaning of the card as symbolizing the cosmos itself. Whenever we give someone a meditation we take part in it ourselves.

At the same time, we can only lead such an exercise with another person after we have gained some experience ourselves. If you are a beginner in meditation you should realize above all that meditation tends to work better the more you do it. If you have never tried it before, it may have a powerful effect the first time you try. More likely, however, you will find it difficult to concentrate, or will simply become physically uncomfortable trying to sit without moving. Keep at it, and if possible go to a teacher for lessons in such basics as breathing and posture.

I am not going to recommend any specific techniques for putting yourself into a meditative state. There are a great many books and classes on this subject, and many people will find they need to try a few before they find the best method that works best for them. Though most of these techniques will adapt themselves to work with Tarot, those which involve visualization (as compared to those emphasizing chanting or total emptiness of mind) will transfer most easily.

Different people use different methods to bring the card into their meditations. Some start with the eyes closed and do not look at the card until they have reached a certain state; others do the opposite. They begin by staring at the card until they reach a certain unity with it, then close their eyes and let the images continue from there. Others hold the card at arm's length, then draw it slowly towards the solar plexus, 'bringing it into the aura'.

However you begin I recommend working with the images and the feelings arising from the card instead of the symbolism you have learned to associate with it. Let the picture affect you, allow your reactions to it to surface and then slide away from you before they block any further experience. I have sometimes found it useful to stare without focussing at the card, so that the symbols and forms dissolve into colour and shape.

At other times, particularly when giving a meditation to someone else, I will ignore the actual picture and suggest some scene associated with it. For instance, for the Fool, instead of that particular person in his multi-coloured suit, I will use a simpler image of a mountain top and clear sunlight. It is more important to set the person, or yourself, in the scene than to follow the card exactly.

Movement or posture can also help to evoke some cards. For the Magician you might stand or sit with one arm raised 'towards heaven' and the other pointing at the earth.

Sometimes the meditation will go no further than an awareness of the card, or a discovery of new ideas about it, and about your self. At other times you will find yourself 'entering' the card, that is, finding yourself within the image, acting out some situation with the figures in the picture. This may happen overwhelmingly, so that you find your whole being *there* instead of *here*. More likely you will experience it as a fantasy unrolling before you, with an awareness at the same time of yourself sitting on the floor or lying on the bed. Either way, it is difficult to describe in words these intense experiences. They carry both a personal and archetypal meaning, for while the cards bear pictures of deepest meaning, what we do with those images comes out of our own needs and experiences.

Various people, such as P. D. Ouspensky and Joseph D'Agostino, have attempted to write down their own Tarot meditations as an example or guide. For me these descriptions do not really convey the experience of the card coming alive, of becoming a part of the picture. Each person will experience different things in these moments. For instance, with Strength you might find yourself running with the lion, or else the woman's flowering wreath might wrap around you, or you might become the woman herself or the lion; or even, as happened to me once, the woman might release the lion to leap at you and claw and bite you.

Here are some more hints. If you do not have a particular image you wish to work with, you can do a reading or simply go through the deck until a card grips you and pulls you into it. Then place it before you and begin with your normal meditation. Become aware of the picture, putting aside any ideas you might have about it. Keep your eyes closed or opened, depending on what works for you; most people find that at least when the fantasy starts they prefer their eyes closed. Try to see and feel yourself in that place with those people and animals.

As mentioned earlier, if you are giving a meditation to someone else you should give them suggestions to get them involved with the image. You may find, after some experiments, that you want to use such suggestions on yourself. For the Hanged Man I often use the image of climbing a great tree, stopping at different levels to look at the land and the sea beneath me, the sky and the stars above. Or you might simply want a description of the card that you can listen to with your eyes closed. If you wish to use such guides you might find it valuable to make a tape ahead of time so that your conscious mind does not have to occupy itself with remembering what comes next. Try to time the tape so that you leave enough silent spaces for yourself to react. You might include the opening of the meditation on the tape, instructing yourself to relax, breathe deeply, etc. or you might simply leave a long silence. Either way, most people prefer to turn the tape on at the beginning and let the instructions come on without their having to make a conscious decision. You can, of course, use the same cassette over and over again, preparing cues for different cards. Or you might make a general tape, with instructions about relaxing, merging with the card, and so on.

Above all, do not try to direct or control what will emerge. This holds for meditations you give to others as well as for yourself. There is a fine line here. Too little direction and the person's attention will drift away; too much and you will not allow the subject's imagination to create its own world. As with other situations, experience is the best guide. For both yourself and others, try not to anticipate, and not to fear, what you experience. Most people do not respect their imaginations enough. They think they can understand whatever their imaginations show them. If they see sudden images of monsters, or devils, or death, they think it means something terrible coming from inside themselves, something they do not wish to face. But the imagination is far more subtle than that. It works in its own way, by its own rules. Often what seems disturbing at first will transform into something inspiring. Jung called the imagination 'the organ of the unconscious'. If you give it its head it will take you where your conscious mind would not have thought – or dared – to go.

All this holds true especially for the Gate cards, as well as the Major ones. Their wordless quality of Strangeness leads us far beyond the literal meanings associated with them. At the same time, because they do represent certain qualities they can also help us achieve those qualities. If it helps to carry a card around it helps even more to carry a Major or Gate card. They are powerful images, with an effect all their own. The act of looking at the Nine of Pentacles, letting it sink into you, helps to *create* discipline, just as carrying and looking at the Six of Pentacles or the High Priestess will help you focus your awareness in a receptive way.

CREATING A 'MANDALA'

So far, we have considered ways to bring the influence of single cards into our lives. But a reading contains many cards which work together. To make a reading come alive, I have found it valuable to create what I call a 'mandala' – a pattern formed from several cards. These cards can include not only those from the reading but others whose qualities will support the direction the reading advises. This act of deliberately adding cards not in the reading extends again the balance between the conscious and the unconscious. The reading has reached into the unconscious areas of knowledge to present a picture of the situation as it exists now. Through the mandala, and through the introduction of new cards deliberately taken from the deck, we can extend or transform the situation.

Here is an example of a mandala in which no extra cards were necessary. The reading itself provided all the images we needed. The following Work Cycle (Fig. 64) concerned a woman who felt isolated from the people around her despite several apparently good friendships.

The Cross illustrated the situation perfectly: Two of Pentacles crossed by Six of Swords. It showed her central situation of pretending to enjoy life and relations with others (Two of Pentacles) producing a sense of functioning ('the swords do not weigh down the boat') while she remained unable to connect with the people around her. She remained like the woman in the boat, wrapped in her shroud, silent.

Briefly, I interpreted the other cards as follows. The Hermit reversed in the position of Past Experience showed the reality of the friendships. At the same time, comparing it with the High Priestess at the end, it suggested she had not learned to use her sense of aloneness creatively, to develop her individuality. The Eight of Swords reversed as the Expectations showed a desire to understand herself and the situation, thereby becoming free of it. It also reflected the political side of the problem, for a good deal of the woman's isolation came from being a member of a minority group, with experiences not shared by any of her friends. At a certain level she was alone. But instead of appreciating her uniqueness among the people around her she allowed herself to hide her own experiences in an attempt to blend in.

The three Work cards were King of Wands reversed, Death

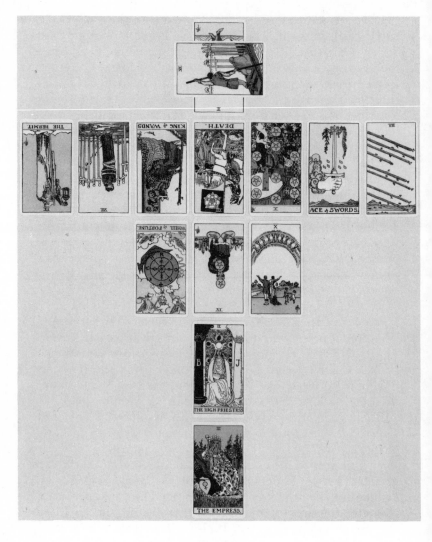

Figure 64
An example of a work cycle reading

reversed, and Ten of Pentacles reversed. The fact that every
card so far had come up reversed; and yet several – such as
Eight of Swords reversed – invited a positive reading, showed
the need for change. The King described an attitude to take
towards herself and others; strong minded, yet tolerant of confusion and weakness. Death reversed, as inertia, indicated a
danger in doing nothing. The need to turn it right side up
became emphasized when we compared it with the Six of
Swords above it. That card shows a journey modelled on the
journey of dead souls. To release herself from the boat of isolation, the sense of a half-life, she would have to complete her
journey by 'dying'; that is, let go of the personality that had
accustomed itself to superficial relationships and inner isolation. The Ten of Pentacles reversed indicated that to do this
she would have to gamble with the security of her current
situation and push her comfortable but limited friendships to
more intense levels.

The Ace of Swords, as the Outcome card showed the strong
attitude as well as the sharp perceptive mind she would need,
and find, to open up the current situation. The Result of this
Outcome, the Eight of Wands, indicated the success of the
gamble. The card carries suggestions of love and friendship. It
symbolizes a journey – the spiritual boat-trip – coming to an
end. Most directly, it signifies the Eight of Swords repression
transformed into positive energy.

We then turned over five more cards in a pattern of three
below the Work cards, then one and one below the Centre.
(There was no special reason for doing this instead of laying
out another line. It was simply an intuitive choice – one that
proved worthwhile.) The three cards gave more attitudes and
approaches to the situation. First, the Wheel of Fortune
reversed indicated the changes she wished to make. The
reversed position suggested difficulties and reinforced the risk
element of the Ten of Pentacles (remember that the Wheel is
also 10). The Four of Pentacles came below Death reversed. It
implied both the idea of releasing energy and of keeping a
structure in her life while she challenged the pattern of her
friendships. The third card continued this meaning. Coming
below the Ten of Pentacles reversed, the Ten of Cups insisted
that while the woman took these risks she must keep an
awareness of the genuine love her friends felt for her. It
referred also to the idea that she must not doubt the person

she lived with, for there she received total support and should answer this gift with trust.

The High Priestess indicated that in a certain sense she would remain alone, for the people around her would still not share her background and experiences. The silence of the High Priestess, however, is not the silence of the Six of Swords. Although silent to others, the High Priestess hints at a strong inner communication, an acceptance and knowledge of the self that a person cannot express in concrete rational terms to other people. The card spoke especially to the woman, who was a poet and had recently written a poem using the metaphor of a private language to express just this idea of deep knowledge available only to oneself.

Below the High Priestess came the Empress, the other side of the feminine archetype. As in the Major Arcana, the two cards complemented each other, for the Empress signified a passionate involvement with life and friendship, not as an opposition to the High Priestess's inner awareness but as a result of it. From a position of self-acceptance the woman could give herself openly to the people around her.

With such a powerful reading the woman wanted to work further with the images. We therefore constructed a mandala for use in meditation and study (see Fig. 65). We began with Death as the centre, for the transformation remained the key. Below Death came the High Priestess on the left, signifying the fact that inner communication must accompany the process for Death to produce real results. The Ace of Swords on the right, stood for sharpness of mind. The Empress went above, to bring about the desired new way of relating to the outside world.

We next placed cards in the four corners around the structure, beginning with the Six of Swords and the Eight of Wands in the bottom left and right. The cards showed the journey and its hoped for end. For the top corners we used the Eight of Swords reversed and the King of Wands reversed – the desired action and the attitude needed to produce it. Finally, as 'legs' for the mandala, we placed the Ten of Cups below the Eight of Wands, and the Ten of Pentacles reversed below the Six of Swords. The images then looked like this:

Figure 65
An example of a mandala

If you have a set of Rider Tarot cards arrange them as in the diagram and look at it for a while. Notice that for meditation you can concentrate on one card, such as Death in the centre, or let the entire pattern sink into the mind, perhaps moving the images about. Since the mandala contains all the elements, with the trumps in the middle, the woman could maintain balance by taking the image into herself.

If you study such an arrangement new relationships emerge between the cards. The Eight of Swords and Eight of Wands are obvious partners; so are the Ten of Cups and Ten of Pentacles reversed. But the Eight of Wands and the King of Wands reversed will also provide new meanings when we consider them together, as do the Eight of Swords reversed and the Six of Swords. Because we have reshaped the reading into a geometric pattern we can draw lines, triangles, etc., constantly discovering new ideas and new patterns. In a way the mandala creates new readings from the same images.

To construct such a pattern, choose the most important cards from the reading and work from the centre out, trying to build the image organically. Place the cards needed for support at the bottom and the cards symbolizing goals at the top. Do not hesitate to introduce cards not found in the original reading if you find a strong need for qualities these cards represent. If you see a need for Temperance, for instance, place it below the centre; or if the reading shows a need for more developed will-power and discipline you might place the Chariot and the Nine of Pentacles side by side above the mandala, as the goal. In this way, you take charge of the reading, opening it to include what your intuition tells you the person needs.

Chapter 8.

What We Learn from Tarot Readings

Most people consult a Tarot reading for specific information. Those who understand the cards a little more may look on the reading as a means of finding a direction. And those who follow a series of readings will see them as a method of keeping in harmony with the changing patterns of life. But to spend a long time reading cards for yourself and others is to discover many things beyond personal information.

We have already seen some of these things. One is people's pessimistic reactions to readings. Another, more important, is the way Tarot readings require – *and therefore create* – a balance between subjective and objective, intuitive and rational, immediate impression and established knowledge, right and left side of the brain. We cannot create such a balance simply by wanting it. We have to let it grow. Tarot readings can help this happen.

But the Tarot teaches us other things as well. It teaches us to pay attention. As we begin to learn the ways in which people act, and the ways in which the world acts on them, we become more and more in the habit of noticing what others do and what we do ourselves. Suppose a person becomes ill whenever a holiday approaches. This could go on for years without the person making the connection and seeing all those illnesses as a subconscious trick to avoid some problem or fear associated with holidays. A Tarot reading can make the person aware of this problem – and makes the reader aware of yet another example of subconscious manoeuvring. Just the practice of reading the Tarot will help us observe these tricks of behaviour, in ourselves as well as in others.

Once we start paying attention to what we do and what happens as a result we notice all sorts of things, not just through readings, but in daily life; patterns of anger and trust, hope and fear, how our response to situations may come from inside us rather than from the situation itself. We become more conscious of the way we deal with work and friends, of tendencies to shift responsibility either *away* from ourselves (It's not fair' or 'You did this to me') or *onto* ourselves ('It's all my fault'). We will notice, for instance, that saying 'It's all my fault' is often a trick to avoid seeing what we have actually done. By making it all or nothing, we make it easy to avoid a true assessment of the situation.

Paying attention makes it just a little bit harder to get depressed or to manipulate other people. As we begin to observe the subtle reasons why people cry or become angry or accuse others, we will at least know a little about ourselves when *we* do these things.

Tarot readings make us aware of the wonderful variety of human nature. As the same cards come up in endless different combinations it becomes clear that people can always produce something new. At the same time, the newness will always come on top of underlying patterns. Through readings we learn in general the ways in which the past affects people, the ways in which their hopes and fears help create the future. But specific past situations and future expectations – these will always surprise us.

Here again we learn the habit of paying attention. For if we start interpreting the cards automatically on the basis of authoritative books or past readings then we lose the truth, and the readings become shallow and confused. Keep a book of past readings, yes, but not simply to use it as examples for future work. Instead, the book can help remind us of the variety and the constant newness of human behaviour.

Notice that, as in creating balance, the Tarot does not simply help us to pay attention. It forces us to do so if we want our readings to produce good results. Tarot readings act as a kind of psychic exercise programme which strengthens the perceptive muscles.

What people do with the information they get from Tarot readings teaches us some important lessons about free will. Many people look on the question of free will as an absolute. Either we make constant choices or we act according to destiny. To give it a more modern context, do we do what we do as a deliberate choice at that moment, or as a result of a lifetime (or many lifetimes) of conditioning?

In terms of Tarot this becomes a practical question. If I act freely at any moment, then how can the cards predict what I will do? What meaning can the reading have if my choice remains totally open until the moment I do something? Or does some power force me to act the way the cards predict?

These problems become easier if we give up the absolute all-or-nothing approach to the question. Then we can say yes, we always retain free will, but we rarely use it. Our conditioning, our past experience, above all our ignorance of all these things, tend to manipulate us in certain directions. The reading reflects these influences and shows their likely result. The cards do not compel the situation to turn out in a certain way. They simply reflect the way in which the influences combine in real life. We can make a diffferent decision when the time comes to act. And yet we do not. Over and over again in life, with little conscious knowledge, we surrender our freedom of choice. We allow our history and conditioning to move us. We do this partly from ignorance, and partly from laziness. It is much easier to follow conditioning than to act on truly conscious decisions.

When I 'failed to follow good advice', when I said to myself, 'Now that I've done the reading I can make sure those bad things won't happen', when I went ahead with my original plan so that the predicted problems arose, I demonstrated how I did not use my free will. I avoided it at the same time that I pretended to be acting on it. This sort of thing happens again and again, and the act of doing Tarot readings shows us very vividly the ways in which people deny their freedom. It is this relationship between freedom and conditioning which forms one of the most valuable pieces of knowledge the Tarot can give us.

The Tarot teaches us as well the valuable lesson of context. No matter how absolute a quality may seem to us in the abstract, in reality it affects us only in the context of other influences. Readings demonstrate this fact in a practical way, as with the woman trying to deal with her lover's jealousy. A card usually thought of as positive, the Sun, actually tended towards a bad result, for by hoping for the Sun she did not face the needs of the situation, and in fact allowed other people's ideas to dictate what she wanted.

Along with context we learn the ways in which the elements

of life balance each other. We see first of all how the suits and specific cards combine to form a unified situation with no suit better or worse than any of the others. Astrologers often find that clients hope for certain signs and elements to dominate their charts, and will show disappointment or even shame if others appear.

Similarly, for some people who know a little about Tarot, if a reading shows a lot of Wands, or Cups, they will feel comforted; if it showed Swords they will become frightened; and if it shows Pentacles they will think of it as trivial, even insulting. Some will only accept a reading which contains many Major cards, because only the trumps, with their implications of power and spiritual awareness, appear important to them.

But even the Major Arcana forms only one element, meaningless without the others. We study it in isolation for its wisdom and powerful description of existence. But in practice we need to mix the spiritual with the mundane, the happy with the sad, love and anger together to understand the world.

The cards teach yet another balance, one hinted at in the scales of Justice. How does the past relate to the future possibilities? How do we combine the effects of our own decision with the influences of the outside world? What do we mean when we say we take responsibility for our lives? Does it mean we create or control everything that happens to us? As in the case of free will many people like to think of responsibility in an absolute way. Either the world shapes us entirely, or we retain total control over our lives. Tarot readings drive home the point that a person's situation at any moment derives from a combination of these things. Just as a very short person cannot expect to become a professional basketball player, so that same person must not consider his whole life dominated by height.

People who accept this idea in theory may still ask: Which counts most – situation or personal responsibility? Which one really controls a person? But Tarot readings demonstrate the meaninglessness of this and similar questions. In some readings the position of Self or Hopes and Fears will clearly dominate. In others Basis or Environment will prove the determining factors. It depends on the person and the particular situation.

Tarot readings help us develop confidence in our own perceptions. Partly this comes from the knowledge gained, and partly from the need to make choices and stick by them. Which of a card's meanings applies in a particular case? Does a court card apply to the subject, some other person, or an abstract principle, such as the King of Swords signifying law and authority, or the Queen of Cups creativity? As we read more we find ourselves starting to sense the answers to these and similar questions. As a result we gain more trust in our understanding and intuition.

What period does a reading cover? With the Celtic Cross or the Work Cycles, the answer can range from a few days to years, not just forwards, but backwards as well. Sometimes, for an adult, the reading can reach back to childhood. The Tree of Life, too, though it usually shows an overview of the whole life, can sometimes show a shorter period if the person is going through a time of intense change.

The different periods of time covered especially in the shorter readings, depend on two things. First, the person's situation and the question asked. Some things, practical or legal matters and certain emotional situations, can bring forth an answer that makes itself apparent within a few days. With others – the working out of emotional conflicts, deep relationships, spiritual or artistic development – it can take a long time before the reading fulfils itself. This does not mean that the readings will not 'come true' for years. We are not speaking of predictions, but of continuing patterns that slowly unfold as time passes.

Second, the different levels a person may touch when mixing the cards. Sometimes he or she may evoke surface situations which last only a short time. At other times the person may mix the cards and somehow go to the very centre of experience. And even here, the reading may show the deep past, or it may reflect the person's potential for future development.

The level reached may not depend at all on the attitude of the person mixing the cards. Usually this approach does make a difference. Someone who sees a reading as a joke or a game will most likely produce a shallow reading; the person who thinks deeply of a question, mixes the cards carefully, and tries to sense the exact moment to stop and cut the deck, will usually produce a reading of some significance. Yet sometimes even such a careful approach will not go below the surface events of the immediate future, while at other times the most casual shuffler will suddenly find her or himself confronted with a powerful image of an entire life. For the reader such moments carry an intense excitement.

Even the question itself may not matter. People can ask about how their work is going, and receive an answer about their new love affair, especially if that question occupies their mind more than the one they asked. Or, as in the case of the woman who found her sexuality blocked by conflicts with her father, the reading may answer the question by bringing up unexpected material from some other area.

How do we know, then, what the reading tells us? Some things become obvious from the images of the cards. If we ask about work and the Lovers and the Two of Cups appear, then the reading will probably concern not work but love. As a beginning reader, however, you cannot expect to uncover all subtleties. Experience alone will help you find your way to the heart of the labyrinth. As you continue with readings you will find yourself able to sense these things. And the heightened perception will carry over to other areas of your life as well.

Sometimes, no matter what our experience or the sharpness of our intuition, we will make mistakes. We might look at the Lovers symbolically when it predicts a love affair with a person the subject still has not met. From this inability to know exactly what the cards mean we can actually learn a very valuable lesson. We become aware of Ignorance. I have capitalized this term because of its essential quality. While most of the knowledge we build up in life is really quite superficial and external, Ignorance lies at the very base of our existence. First of all, we are ignorant of the true nature of things. What we know of the world is bounded by our sense organs. For us to see the words on this page, light must bounce off them to be collected by our eyes. Then the optic nerve carries impulses to the brain, which converts the impulses into others, arranging them into meaningful patterns our consciousness understands as language. But we cannot directly know, in the sense of merging with something out there. We can only convert the universe into impulses, patterns, symbols.

Similarly, because we exist in physical form, we must work out our lives in the boundaries of time. This means, among other things, that we cannot realize all our potential, because we must always choose to do one thing and not another with the few years available to us. A person with the ability to become both a dancer and a businessman will have to choose one over the other. And which ever he chooses he will have to work for years before he can actually achieve his goal. Time means also that we often cannot know the consequences of actions we take, simply because the consequences might not appear until years in the future. Sometimes the consequences of our actions appear not to us but to other people. Something we do in a certain place may affect people there long after we have moved, or even died. Quite simply, time means things must happen before we can know about them.

Meditation with the Eight of Swords as a Gate can increase our awareness of Ignorance. Tarot readings – and the mistakes we make as we try to interpret them – can demonstrate Ignorance more directly. A Tarot reading actually reaches beyond time, bringing out the true pattern that includes past and future. The random pattern of the cards leads us to bypass the limitations of consciousness. And yet that limited consciousness must interpret the reading. Therefore, at one and the same time, we experience the true state of the universe, in which all things exist together, and our own extremely limited time-bound knowledge of it. We experience both truth and ignorance.

The other side of Ignorance is Certitude, the state of knowing reality, rather than the impressions and symbols our limited consciousness forms from it. Many people consider ecstasy, or oneness with the light of God, as the supreme goal of the mystic or occultist. But as the Major Arcana of the Tarot demonstrates, the lightning bolt of ecstasy forms only a step along the way. The true goal is Certitude, the state of knowing where before we could only guess.

What is the real cause of any single action? What will its consequences be, not just to the person who has acted, but to others, both known and unknown? Those few people who have achieved Certitude can see the causes and consequences within the action itself. The rest of us can only guess about these and a thousand other things. We remain Ignorant.

But even if we cannot guess at the true interpretation of a Tarot reading, the reading itself reaches beyond that time-bound Ignorant state. The reading carries Certitude, if not the reader. And if we work enough with cards, comparing our interpretations with subsequent events, becoming more and more involved with the pictures, developing our intuition, then sometimes we can get experiences of Certitude, of knowing the true meaning of something. While such experiences carry their own value, they serve us most by giving us a sense of direction. They help us perceive what we want to achieve.

Finally, the practice of Tarot reading teaches us something else. Because the cards are not neutral in their attitude to life, because they embody certain approaches and beliefs, and renounce others, they change us. We begin over time – always over time – to see the balance of things, the steady harmony within the constant shift and flow of life. We become aware of the Strangeness always waiting beyond our ordinary experience, we learn to recognize the gifts we receive from existence, and our own responsibility to understand and use them. Most of all, we begin to grasp the truth the Tarot always urges upon us – that the universe the whole universe, lives. And what we can know of ourselves we can know of everything.

Index